To JOE —
ON OUR ONLY VICTORY
SINCE '75.

Vikings — ONWARD &
Upward
JOE
SAC

THEY'RE PLAYING MY GAME

THEY'RE PLAYING MY GAME

HANK STRAM
with LOU SAHADI

WILLIAM MORROW AND COMPANY, INC.
NEW YORK

Library of Congress Cataloging-in-Publication Data

Stram, Hank.
    They're playing my game.

    1. Stram, Hank.   2. Sportscasters—United States—
Biography.   3. Football—United States.   I. Sahadi, Lou.
II. Title.   III. Title: They are playing my game.
GV742.42.S77A3   1986   070.4'49796'0294 [B]   86-12527
ISBN 0-688-06080-3

Printed in the United States of America

First Edition

1 2 3 4 5 6 7 8 9 10

BOOK DESIGN BY RICHARD ORIOLO

To my wife, Phyllis,
my sons Henry, Dale, Stu, Gary,
my daughters Julia, Mary,
my mother,
my sister,
my Aunt Mary.

THEY'RE PLAYING MY GAME

ONE

I was closing out the season in Los Angeles covering the play-off game between the Los Angeles Rams and the Dallas Cowboys for CBS television. From high above the playing field I took in the symmetry of the offensive line's rumps. Two fannies, I thought, were farther back from the line of scrimmage than the others. The two guards were cheating—giving themselves a barely discernible jump on the action with a few finessed inches. My hunch was they were going to pull out of their positions and roar off to lead the play. Okay, but which way?

As a football coach I spent a lot of time studying peoples' backsides. As a sportscaster I am similarly preoccupied. It is not an idle interest, but more a professional obsession. Such hindsight, if you will, can prompt the knowledgeable observer to considerable foresight. It is not quite like reading tea leaves or divining for water, but the leeward side of an offensive line *can* tell you quite a lot about what is going to happen in the next few seconds. Which was something I badly needed to know because beside me, in the booth, Jack Buck was finishing his comments on the instant replay of the previous down. After a dozen years of working together I didn't even need to look at him to know I was about to get the handoff. I glanced instead at the split backfield.

The formation was good for a pass, draw or screen. The big halfback was positioned on the right. Few teams have two big men in the backfield. Ninety-five percent of the time the big guy will do the blocking, the smaller back will run. In this instance the bigger man was not exactly even with his colleague. He was closer to the line than the smaller back: "cheating up," buying himself an extra fraction of a second to do his job by being closer to his target across the way. Probably he was to hit the linebacker or defensive end.

The small back, meanwhile, is a half-step farther to his left than usual. Why? Because he is giving the burly guard, on his side of the line, extra room to pull out and lead the way across the formation. A run to the right is my guess.

Jack Buck preps me, gives me the lead-in. The quarterback is in his audible, calling out a color that, by prearrangement, will either confirm the play already set in the huddle or will substitute the new one he is now shouting out. No one shifts. I quietly predict a run to the right side.

The quarterback barks the count and the ball is immediately snapped. The play goes right: a run, the guards leading, Jack nods. That's one for our team.

Around us dozens of reporters are poised over their writing machines and microphones. Eyes and TV cameras follow the action upfield, all except the camera fixed on the bench of the team opposite our vantage point. Its operator keeps the viewfinder trained on the far sideline and the zoom tight on the two assistants who motion signals to the quarterback on the field. One of them is really signaling, the other is a decoy. Both are being filmed.

Later the footage of their signals will be painstakingly matched with the plays to which they correspond, then analyzed, cross-referenced, and the signals decoded. The next time against this particular opponent there will be surprises perhaps.

No one in the press box gives the camera a moment's thought. Its twin no doubt is somewhere on the other rim of the stadium performing a similar chore for the other team. Skunking it's called. It is an integral part of the endless game of winning games, as honorable as military intelligence, a kind of one-upmanship that had been in the game since the beginning, since Jim Thorpe first tucked sheet metal into his shoulder pads to give his hits that extra little zing.

As games go, this one wasn't a rout, a blowout, but the Rams weren't exactly taxed either. I was feeling a little let down as the gun sounded. I always did at the end of a season. So Jack and I took off for Las Vegas and made it in time to catch the gala Saturday night show of an old friend, Bobby Vinton. It was a splendid way to finish up . . . almost.

The next morning we flew to St. Louis for our regular two-hour radio talk show on the NFL. Then, finally, we parted, and I headed home to Covington, Louisiana, and my family.

Our house sits on fifteen acres in a secluded spot fast by the bayou of the Tchefuncte River, about twenty-five miles from the wonderful city of New Orleans and the Gulf of Mexico beyond. It is wooded and peaceful, and I looked forward to spending some time with Phyllis and the kids after covering four preseason games and fifteen league games in nearly as many states on network television and doing twenty-six two-hour radio broadcasts of our football call-in show. They hadn't called me "Hurryin' Henry" in high school for nothing.

The postseason lull was further delayed by the Super Bowl. It was coming to New Orleans this year and bringing with it all the attendant excitement. I had to see it, of course, and a lot of old friends like Roger and Pam Stanton. For the two weeks prior to the game they kept dropping by, or we met them in the city at Jimmy Moran's Riverside Restaurant, where most of the sports people tended to gather. Impromptu reunions took place there every night. There also was a roast for ex-Saint Archie Manning, Senator Jack Kemp's testimonial brunch (the former quarterback was running for president), an elegant cocktail party in Chris Owens's lavish home in the French Quarter with Wilson and Mikki Abraham, the National Football League party, the New England Patriots brunch, and, wedged in among them, eight speeches I had to make. Every moment seemed filled, right up to the opening ceremonies of the game itself.

Super Bowl XX. I had the afternoon off for a change, at least from televising duties (Jack and I were scheduled for a post-game radio show). The "other" network was televising the game this year, so I could sit in the stands like a fan and enjoy most of the fray: the Chicago Bears versus the New England Patriots. Accepting the gracious invitation of Raiders owner Al Davis, my wife and I joined him in a luxurious skybox high above the emerald-green field on which I had coached my last game a decade earlier. I looked around the box. Chargers owner Alex Spanos was there as well. Also Baron Hilton, Jimmy "the Greek" Snyder, Coach George Allen, Bob Oates of the *Los Angeles Times*.

I stared up at the elliptical roof overhead, then scanned the pristine expanse of synthetic turf below. The sidelines were crowded with hundreds of photographers, broadcasting gear, medical equipment, ambulances, doctors and paramedics, radio phones, cables, football equipment, officials in their black-and-white uniforms, cheerleaders, security guards, TV cameramen, celebrities, and NFL officials. The Superdome was jammed as well. Seats, officially seventy-five dollars, were changing hands for many hundreds. Funny, I thought. When I coached my first Super Bowl game in 1967, a third of the stadium sat empty. In those days tickets costs from six to twelve dollars apiece. CBS and NBC had jointly paid an unprecedented two-million-dollar fee to simultaneously telecast Super Bowl I over both networks. It was a sum that wouldn't have bought a two-minute spot on Super Bowl XX.

Twenty seasons had passed since I coached the Kansas City Chiefs against Vince Lombardi's legendary Packers in that first Super Bowl. It felt like twenty minutes. Vince Lombardi. His team was like him—a sledgehammer. Nothing fancy. No frills, no gadgets, just a straight-ahead attack designed to run over or through you. His uncompromising nature left its mark on pro football and had come to symbolize the flintheadedness required to survive in the game. Appropriately enough, a few years after his death his name was bestowed upon the Super Bowl award itself, and so the latest winners would receive a Tiffany-crafted Lombardi Trophy of sterling silver.

10

It was nearing game time. The Most Valuable Players of past championships were introduced, among them Len Dawson, Kansas City quarterback. He was among the finalists in the Hall of Fame balloting scheduled for that coming week and I was very proud of him.

The captains met at midfield. The officials walked them through the mock coin toss and designated the goals to be defended, the team to receive the kick. The captains shook hands all around and turned quickly back to their respective benches. The crowd roared. Moments later the ball arched through the air and the game was on.

As different as the setting was from that of the first Super Bowl in Los Angeles, it became oddly familiar to me as the Bears' offensive team came to the line and set up in the I-formation, which I had introduced to the pros in the early sixties. Stranger still, the Patriots lined up opposite them in an odd-man 3-4 defense—another formation the Chiefs had introduced.

I swiveled around in my plush seat and looked at the composed faces of the other guests. The TV monitors overhead were carrying the network coverage. There was not a smirk on anyone's face or a disparaging comment about the formations being bush league or unworkably complex. How times had changed, I thought.

Back when I first used them, people thought I was plain crazy. They responded to these same formations with open disdain, as if we had introduced something malodorous. Now no one said a word; my heresies had become not only acceptable but normal. The moving pocket, the camouflaged slot, the double tight end, man-in-motion, set shift—once these had all been scorned as flimflam. Today they were even respectable. The arsenals of the NFL were loaded with them.

A roar went up. The Bears fumbled and lost the ball on their own 19-yard line. It looked like a great opportunity for the Patriots. If they could just beat Chicago's 46 defense.

The 46 was already the stuff of legends and said to be terribly complex. Actually it was as simple as a blunt instrument and, like most things in football, it depended entirely on the talent of those who executed the scheme to make it successful. Its aim was to stop the run at all costs by overloading the line, battering through the offense at high speed, and shooting into the backfield. It worked especially well against the open formations so conducive to the passing game football had become. Nonetheless, there was a way to beat it.

The 46 conceded the opposition a lot of passing opportunities. The only trick was to capitalize on them even as some of the fiercest defensive players in the league charged in at you. It was a race to see who would connect first—a receiver with the ball, or a defender with the quarterback. If you had the people to make it work, it worked brilliantly. If you didn't—like the Atlanta Falcons, who had tried it—then it failed totally. An aggressive, gambling kind of defense it was, and exciting to watch.

Tony Eason, the Patriots' young quarterback, brought his team to the line for their first play of the game. A pass! It was unconventional, unexpected, and the right call, except the end didn't catch it. Had he, the Patriots would have looked like geniuses.

On second down the quarterback threw again, a quick slant over the middle that was right on the money, but the receiver dropped it. The Patriots regrouped and huddled. The element of surprise was gone; with third down and the full 10 yards needed to have the chance of another series, everyone in the stadium knew a pass was coming. If the Patriots intended to keep on throwing, there could be dire consequences. Also, I noticed that their quarterback was dropping straight back instead of rolling out, away from the onrushing linemen.

Of the nineteen quarterbacks who had won in the Super Bowl, sixteen were movers. The only straight drop-back passers were Bart Starr, who won the first two, and Joe Namath in the third. Then came the Chiefs' Len Dawson, working out of a moving pocket. All the succeeding winners moved, with the exception of Kenny Stabler in 1977, and he was an ex-scrambler who had just gotten banged up too much to run around.

Could those three great drop-back quarterbacks win today?

It was a question I didn't want to think about as I watched the Bears defense deploy. Who could imagine pro football without Joe Namath, for instance? I didn't care to contemplate how he and those fragile knees of his would have fared against the pass rush that was destroying the Patriots' quarterback before our very eyes. Chicago's defensive innovations were effective as hell, and the Patriots were out of the game by their third possession.

Football in the eighties had become basketball on grass, a game of push-and-shove, and pick-and-go. The reason for this is simple: a rules change that legalized holding on offense. Most changes in the nature of the game, however, originate in the imaginations of the men confined to the sidelines. The one we were admiring, the 46, was Coach Buddy Ryan's.

As it turned out, the Bears were nearly as daring on offense as on defense. They were slugging away like heavyweights; the Patriots were reeling. Their quarterback, Jim McMahon, played with an abandon that reminded me of Joe Kapp when we faced him and the Vikings in Super Bowl IV. This guy was a combatant.

I listened to the voices of the commentators on the TV monitors and thought back to the time I had left coaching for broadcasting. It hadn't been easy. After forty years of playing and coaching, I certainly knew the sport that I had fallen in love with as a grade-schooler. Talking about it to millions of people on television and radio was a whole other thing, however; so was having a director talk at you on your earphones even while you were talking to the folks at home. That was an alien sensation, and more than once I made the mistake of answering the whisper in my ear as if it were a voice the audience could also hear.

When I started broadcasting it was rugged. Basically, they just tossed me in and told me, "Do it." "When you see the red light go on, start talking," is how they put it. "Do it your way," was their advice. And I did. Mostly there wasn't much choice. Now it is much more organized and directed, and I am an old hand with lots of experience.

During the season I read up on the next team every day, watch film, learn names, the numbers they go with, the personalities of the guys wearing the uniforms. For a Sunday telecast, I arrive on the preceding Friday morning and go straight to the stadium to meet with the team's PR director. Then it's down to the practice to see the team work out and compare notes with producer Mike Arnold or Bob Stenner, and director Bob Dunphy or Bob Fishman. A lot of planning is done standing up, in brief exchanges as we move about the edges of the practice session. Afterward I look at more film and talk to everyone I can. If the air gets too thick with the usual buzz words or contradictory rumors, I seek out the guys who know the team intimately and always give it to you straight—the trainers and the equipment men. Often they have the best information and insights, like trainer Eddie Abramoski of the Bills.

A few seasons back the rumors were rife that the head coach was about to be fired because the team hadn't won a game all season and wasn't likely to that coming Sunday against the Cowboys. Eddie disagreed. The team, he insisted, was up. Practices had been terrific all week, and the players thought their coach was getting it done, preparing them well, and that they had a good future with him at the helm.

"Don't be surprised if they beat Dallas," Eddie said. "I'd bet they will."

I conveyed Ed Abramoski's views to the public on the pregame segment that Sunday and, sure enough, the Bills defeated the vaunted Cowboys.

Teams are mysterious. It is easy to talk about them in terms of attitude and discipline and the like, but few collections of individuals actually earn the right to call themselves a team. Few people understand what makes a team tick, what makes it go. Sometimes even great coaches, like the Patriots' Raymond Berry, cannot stop a fine team from unraveling.

I winced as the Bears scored again. It wasn't New England's day. Despite the shellacking, the Patriots' veteran defenseman, Julius Adams, wasn't letting up even though he was retiring afterward. For everyone else on the field it was the last game of the season. For him it was the last game of his life. Although it was already lost, he was not going to quit. Adams drove forward and banged into the Bears offensive line with the abandon of a rookie.

The game changes, the real players don't.

TWO

SHERRILL Headrick with a hemorrhoid cushion on his head, one of those inflatable doughnut things, sitting in the back of a plane with his teammates, laughing. That's what it's about—guys like him.

When I was putting together my first pro-football team for the 1960 season, Sherrill was a highly publicized linebacker out of TCU. I had never seen him play, but I'd heard lots about him over the years. When our scout, Willie Walls, had the good fortune to sign him for the team, I was delighted. When he walked into my office a few days later, I despaired.

The legendary Sherrill Headrick had a little potbelly, no muscular definition, and was just average size. He didn't look anything like the player you would have expected, given his fearsome reputation. It didn't take long to learn I had been presumptuous. Headrick came to practice and drove us crazy.

He would watch the offensive center and the two guards, and—depending on how much weight they'd put on their hands at the line of scrimmage—he could tell just where the play was going to go, and he would deliver himself there in a devastating manner. We had a hell of a time simply running through plays. No matter what we tried, we never could deceive him. He had an unfailing sense of where the ball was headed and what angle he might take to interdict it. Great football smarts. He was a great bridge player too, which should have tipped me to how savvy a linebacker he might be. He was the most instinctive I've ever seen.

And a very gregarious fellow off the field, always clowning. If I announced a test on the airplane (meaning, a test of new plays on the way to a game), invariably Sherrill would pipe up, "Coach, I don't rightly know anything about airplanes." But, as easygoing as he was, something came over him before every game. We could never take the field until we heard him finish throwing up in the bathroom. The whole team kind of hung around until he got through with the sound effects, and only when he was done did we leave the dressing room. It's just something we did as a matter of course before every game: We waited for Sherrill to throw up.

You couldn't imagine a more charged-up competitor, or one who would play with more pain. I don't know how many times he came to the sideline with dislocated or broken fingers, got the trainer to set them and tape 'em up, and back in he'd go. He played a whole game once with what turned out to be a cracked vertebra. One week, when his chronic hemorrhoids suddenly required immediate surgery, I thought that was it: He would finally miss a game. Thursday they operated. He was supposed to stay in the hospital to recuperate, but Saturday we boarded our plane to California, and so did Sherrill.

We had a five-hour flight out to Oakland, and just sitting there, even on his doughnut cushion, must have been excruciating, though you wouldn't have known it from looking at him. The next afternoon he suited up and played one of his finest games. Sherrill Headrick never played a bad game in his life, but that Sunday he was spectacular. And on the way home, there he was, sitting up in the back part of the plane where the boys played cards, that inflated cushion on his head like a halo, leading the cheers all the way to Texas.

Most people worry about not losing. Only a few, like Sherrill, concentrate on winning. He just loved it. Oh, he loved to play, he loved the combat and the tension, but most of all he liked to win. Sounds simple. It isn't. And yet it's at the heart of it all if you're an athlete. Sure, winning is what you got paid to do as a pro, but that wasn't what made you go for it. Heck, in those days nobody got paid all that much anyway, by today's standards.

No, it wasn't anything so simple as the money, or as uncomplicated as a burning desire, or a temporary high, or some kind of mellow satisfaction that got better with age. For the few like Sherrill, winning was an all-consuming passion that could make your best friend or former teammate your worst enemy. I know. One of my best friends in football is Al Davis.

When Al took over the Oakland Raiders in 1963, they were the doormat of the American Football League. They couldn't beat anybody. They probably couldn't have won an intra-squad scrimmage. In two years they had won three whole games. Then, bang! In one season they're 10 and 4, and Al is Coach of the Year. And the Raiders are suddenly a pain in the ass. From then on, whenever the Kansas City Chiefs went to Oakland to play the Raiders, I knew we were in for it.

My team arrived neatly attired in tailor-made, identical black blazers and gray slacks, white shirts and black ties, with the team emblem emblazoned on the breast pocket and tie. Their hair was neatly cut, their faces clean-shaven, as the club rules required—no facial hair, no long sideburns. Precision and style were our trademarks on and off the field. Multiple offenses, exact execution, innovative play, discipline.

How we looked when we traveled, how we played, how we lined up for the national anthem, were all in keeping with our determination to be a first-class, big-league team. We were representing the new American Football League and our city. We had a distinct personality that we wanted to be known. So did the Oakland Raiders.

A lot of them were what coaches call "attitude problems," guys who won't go along with the precepts laid down by the management. You know, rugged individuals who chafed at the strict conformity and endless repetition demanded by the game. As a result, most of the Raiders had bounced from one team to another like bad checks. Al offered them a haven. At first, no one thought he could control such a collection of rowdies, but they don't call Al "the Genius" for nothing. He didn't even try. He let two things do it for him: their pride in their own superiority, and the slow realization, which he just let sink in, that this was probably their last stop in the pros. If they were going to make it in big-time football, they'd have to make it with the Raiders. It was their last shot. Al's only rule was *win*!

They began to call themselves the Foreign Legion, and they looked it. Protruding from their helmets were beards, moustaches, long hair. They were one fierce bunch of scruffy mavericks, made all the tougher by Al Davis's ingenious design. What others had judged as negative, he converted into positive strength and a motivation for winning big. Luck may be a lady, he seemed to say to them, but winners aren't always gents.

My players would cautiously enter the visitors' dressing rooms down in the bowels of Oakland Coliseum, their brows furrowed at the sight of the gritty facilities. The locker area was cramped, damp, and just plain lousy. Likewise, the field was always sloppy and wet, which suited the Raiders just fine.

It had been built on a landfill and had a peculiar odor. This probably accounted for the mushy, moist texture of the turf, but other teams invariably suspected the Raiders of wetting the field because it favored the home team's style of play. The Oakland teams were straight-ahead, power types, big and strong, and happy as pigs in mud on their slow field. And I mean mud. One of our players, Jim Tyrer, weighing 290 pounds, once ran out of his shoes on that field. The mud just sucked them off. He couldn't find them after the play. They weren't found, in fact, until the following spring when the field was plowed.

When Oakland came to play at Municipal Stadium in Kansas City, I would do my best to reciprocate their hospitality. I doubted that even rats' nests in their locker room would've given them pause. However, I knew the Legion of the Damned was dead serious about football. Make the field hard as a rock, I told grounds keeper George Toma, so it would favor our speed. George wouldn't let anybody so much as spit on the grass. But even with the home-field advantage, Al Davis's club was hard to handle. He had infused them with that tremendous drive of his to win.

Brains help in leading a team; so does having a strategic mind; and you also must have an ego that won't crumble when you don't win. But really, in pro football one squad is not that much superior to any other in terms of latent talent. What makes the difference is that spark of passion, and the coach's ability to pressure or coax it out of players then aim it at that other team. Sure, you count on a basic love of the game being there in everyone involved, and on the desire of people to succeed, but what you look for constantly are the rare ones who want to own the outcome, the ones who almost need it. Like Al Davis.

Cards, golf, business, tiddlywinks—it doesn't matter the game, Al must win at it. Being as smart as he is, he will inevitably win financially and artistically (that's right, I said *artistically*). But if you somehow forced him to choose between the money, stock options, bonuses, equity, and simply winning—just winning—it would be no contest.

He is a master at motivating others to want it because he wants it so badly himself. He knows just how sweet and seductive it can be, and how nothing the alternative is. Maybe Al and I are friends because we are much alike in this respect.

People ask me what the difference is between broadcasting games, which I love, and coaching. The answer is simple: winning. Walking out of the booth after one of the league games I cover each season, that feeling isn't there anymore. I don't know if I've "won" or "lost," and for a long time that was the hardest thing to get used to. It is, after all, something you experience from childhood on if you're seriously involved in athletics, and it's the thing around which your life centers for a very long time, season after season. Which is great, if you're a competitor—but not always, because if it gets too powerful, it begins to lead you more than you direct it. Certainly, it gave me the stamina to deal with the pressures and demands of coaching. As with all of one's strengths, however, they are also, at once, your weaknesses.

In 1969, I had the good fortune to sign an exceptional young player, Mike Garrett, for the Kansas City Chiefs. We scooped every other team and got him because they thought he was too small, even though he had won the Heisman Trophy as the best college player. We took the gamble on his skills, and it paid off brilliantly, yet I almost blew it over a Ping-Pong match.

It was in the basement of our home in Shawnee Mission, Kansas. He came to a team party, his first, and he and I got into a deadly Ping-Pong game. He didn't know it, but it was something I did with a lot of new prospects just to see how they competed if their concentration was disrupted. At 180 pounds and five feet eight inches, he was about my size. I had even played the same position as Mike in high school and college. Anyhow, we were locked up in a savage contest. He was really into winning it and so was I.

The basement had a low ceiling. I slammed the ball off it and onto his side of the net. Point for me. During the next volley, I hit the ball off the side wall with similar success and won, infuriating the young man. Moreover, I could see he deeply resented the way I had won.

I should have explained to Mike why I had played in this manner and that there was a lesson to be learned from it, and that no one could promise him football would be fair. At best it's a series of advances and setbacks. It's not a question of whether you are going to get beaten sometimes, just whether you bounce back. If you win more than you lose, if you get up more times than you go down, you will succeed. That's what it was about if you were a pro. I should have explained, but I didn't.

A small, dumb incident is what it was, but it ate at our relationship, I thought. The young man had been initiated that night in some way; I could sense it. But he hadn't liked it at all. If getting taken in a Ping-Pong game was going to throw him, I wondered how he would do on the field. As it turned out, he was spectacular. Years later, though, he asked to be traded, and I always thought it was because of that Ping-Pong match.

The truth was that I didn't know how to play a game without

caring deeply about winning. I was good at it—damn good—and had been for as long as I could remember: in track, basketball, as a pitcher, as captain of my high school football team, and as All-State halfback. Once you were on the field, in the arena, on the court, the track, whatever—that was it. Win! When winning wasn't the object, I found it terribly annoying. Like in preseason games.

The object of preseason games against other clubs was to test new personnel, to get a look at newcomers and test what they could do. Ours became a charade. Every spring I vowed not to succumb to my urges, and every summer I did.

Before each preseason game I would instruct my staff to make sure we substituted early so the new guys got a chance to show their stuff. My assistants were to yank my sleeve, if necessary, and make sure it happened. And they would. They almost tore the arms off my sports coat. Invariably, I'd play my best veterans and stay with them as I got wrapped up in the game itself, and the new team members and rookies rarely got a proper chance as a result.

Annoyed with myself afterward, I'd snap at the reporters: "It may be just an exhibition game, but nobody will ever convince me it's good to lose." The rationale had some merit. We wore our work clothes, our numbered jerseys, pads, helmets, so why not play to win? Establishing a winning habit early in a season wasn't unreasonable, it just wasn't completely true. The truth was, I liked to win. Play was something you did for its own sake, but play was for children. This was no game. It wasn't completely grown-up, but it was totally serious. It had little to do with money and everything to do with winning. Like lemon meringue pie, I loved it when I had it and worried about it afterward . . . sometimes. What else was there, after all?

At the end of the film version of General Patton's life, he's an old man walking his dog, and the voice on the screen says how in ancient Rome, when a general came home victorious, he was received with a tremendous parade. But beside him on his chariot, holding the Wreath of Victory above his head, stood a slave who'd whisper all along the route, "Victory is fleeting. Victory is fleeting."

Hell, the Roman Empire might have lasted longer if they had used Sherrill Headrick's hemorrhoid cushion instead, and repeated into the general's ear what I've heard Al Davis whisper to Raider players so often: "Win, baby. Just win!"

I think I came by my obsession naturally, from being exposed as a kid to some very determined athletes. One was Tony Zaleski, a prizefighter. Tony was one of five brothers, all of whom worked in the Gary, Indiana, steel mills.

He had been a great amateur boxer. When he turned pro, he lost a string of fights and went to work in the mills for a year. When I was ten, he came over one night to talk to my dad about it, and he sat in a chair and cried because he just knew he could do it and wanted it so bad. Dad encouraged his friend. Tony resumed boxing and began winning. He was a terrific puncher. In 1941, he went to Seattle and won the middleweight championship of the world from Al Hostak. He came back by train, and we all met him at the station, along with most of Gary. Everyone turned out to see "the Man of Steel." It was one of the most thrilling things I'd seen.

His next challenger was Rocky Graziano. Tony beat him—actually knocked him out in the sixth round in New York—but lost their second fight some months later. I'll never forget going to the YMCA in Gary with my pal, Julie Rykovich, and running into Tony, who was training for the rematch and still steaming from the loss.

"I will fight him in an alley. I will fight him in a locker room. I will fight him in a phone booth. I will fight him for nothing, but I want my title back." And he meant it.

The rematch was set: Tony Zale (his ring name) versus Rocky Graziano. It was fought in New Jersey, and Tony Zale knocked out the Rock in the third round and took back his crown.

My father was very athletic too. As a young Polish immigrant, he had challenged the Barnum & Bailey wrestling champion to a match and beat him. He so impressed the crowd that the circus signed him up to replace their fallen champ. He traveled with them for a while, and somewhere along the way assumed the name Stram for his real one, Wilczek. He was a very exuberant, outgoing man and became a salesman for a custom-made clothing company in Chicago, but he never stopped wrestling and participating in sports.

However, the local hero who most influenced me was an older boy who played for a rival high school on the north side. His name was Tommy Harmon.

THREE

GLEASON Field was the big time. All the schools in Gary played there. It was quite a place. On one side were the steel mills and on the other the rail lines that wound into Chicago. Often the trainmen would stop there and watch games in progress. If the wind blew from the north, we'd get smoke from the mills; if it blew from the south we'd get smoke from the trains. For the first week of the season it was a grass field; after that, rock-hard dirt.

Gleason Field is where I watched Tommy Harmon play football every chance I got. He was a senior at Horace Mann on the north side, I was a freshman at Lew Wallace on the south side. He was All-State in football, basketball, and track—a genuine sensation—and I would go to his every game and watch him practice whenever I could. In the summer, when he worked at the beach on Lake Michigan as a lifeguard, I would even go out to watch him run back and forth in the soft sand to get his legs in shape.

He went on to great fame, of course, first as a college player and winner of the Heisman Trophy, and then as a pro with the Los Angeles Rams, making famous the 98 he wore on his jersey throughout his long career.

Watching him play for Horace Mann High was a bright moment in my freshman year, which was otherwise dark. My father had just died, and my mother opened a little restaurant to support my sister, Dolly, and me. Every morning she would wake me at five o'clock and get me off to school. I hitchhiked or jogged the five miles past the mills and caught a streetcar that took me the remaining ten to school.

I played halfback for two years before my mother even knew I was participating in football. She found out accidentally one day when my picture appeared in the paper. We talked about it that night, and I confessed that I'd gotten my sister to sign the required parental permission slip, because I knew my mother wouldn't have. My father had encouraged me in other sports but never liked football. She knew that, of course, and asked me to quit the team, but I pleaded with her that football was the game I loved most and most wanted to play. She hugged me and said, "Then do the best job you can."

From that night on she came to watch all my games and cheered me on as I became an All-State halfback, even though never for an instant did she have the slightest understanding of what she was watching.

Tony Zale and Tommy Harmon were incredibly important to us when we were growing up. Mostly you just heard about the great players, read about them in the newspapers, or glimpsed them in the newsreels. But there was no television, and you never really saw them play, so you had the peculiar feeling that they weren't really people. To see a Tony Zale, a Tom Harmon, was incredible, because you saw that they weren't that different from you, and that if you wanted it badly enough, there was a chance you could make it.

Me, I wanted it bad. I lettered in football, basketball, track, and baseball, and went to Purdue, in West Lafayette, Indiana, on a football scholarship. I was five feet seven and only 155 pounds, but Purdue used me as a tailback, and I became a starter my sophomore year, 1942. Amazingly enough, I was even invited to play in the College All-Star game and would've loved to play in it, but Uncle Sam had other plans for me and many of my classmates.

Three years later I went back to play for a new coach, Cecil Isbell, as a halfback in the T-formation. Flooded with guys studying on the GI Bill, the little university was now a small city. Anyway, I earned back my spot on the team and immersed myself in studying and playing. I had notebooks full of plays and besieged Pinky Wilson and the other coaches with variations on the plays we were using. The strategizing really caught my imagination.

A bad ankle injury hobbled my football career, and I was unhappy with my performance, but in my senior year I was surprised with the Big Ten Medal, which was the prize for the best all-around athlete-scholar. It was a wonderful finish to my days at Purdue, and completely unexpected because I had played for four different coaches in four years. All that remained was to figure out how I'd live after graduation, which was fast approaching. A friend talked me into taking the test for the FBI and I passed, only to find that the Bureau had added a law-degree requirement before I could take my federal vows and join J. Edgar's silent ranks of G-men.

Then out of the firmament came a summons to Head Coach Stu Holcomb's office and an offer to become the first assistant coach enlisted from the graduating classes at Purdue, a one-year internship they had just instituted. Was I happy! So was my love, Phyllis.

I had met her in sociology class. She was a drum majorette and lived right across the street from the field house. She was very energetic and talented: She sang with a swing band, had her own radio show on campus, gave baton lessons, and was an excellent student.

To expand my annual salary of thirty-six hundred dollars, I played baseball for the Fort Wayne General Electrics, who had been the champions of the Indiana-Michigan league under manager John Braden the previous year. I got four hundred dollars a month and another hundred for expenses, which was great. What wasn't so great was that they played nearly every night against the Indianapolis Clowns, Homestead Greys, South Bend Studebakers, Kansas City Monarchs, and St. Joe Oscos.

Phyllis, teammate John Chinswicz, and I would leave at noon, after graduate classes, and head for Fort Wayne, Michigan City, or wherever. We'd play the game at eight, leave the stadium at one in the morning, jump back in the car, and drive home another two or three hours.

The next morning I'd rush off to my early classes, pick up Phyllis and John at lunchtime, and head out again. Phyllis and I were madly in love and terribly young, but I was glad when the baseball season ended and my job on the coaching staff began.

That was 1948. We began our season against Frank Leahy's great Notre Dame team. It was a nationally televised game, and the Fighting Irish were heavily favored. They won too—but just barely, by a single point. It was a truly magnificent game. Our quarterback, Bob DeMoss, threw four touchdown passes, and the final score was 28–27. Naturally, we got a lot of press and invitations.

When Stu Holcomb turned out to have a conflicting speaking engagement, I was sent to address a group in Chicago and show the game film. I was scared to death, but Stu said, "Just narrate the film, say something, and answer the questions. Don't worry about it, that's all there is to it."

The audience of the Chicago Quarterback Club turned out to include Bo McMillan, head coach of the Detroit Lions; Sid Luckman, the quarterback of the Chicago Bears; and George Halas, the man who invented modern professional football. Oh, and about one thousand earnest fans.

My knees were knocking, but I was also more excited than I had ever been in my life as I answered their questions about our team. From then on I was often to be found driving somewhere in my best blue suit, with a film of one of our games on the seat beside me. I didn't mind at all; I liked it.

The following year Leahy took no chances with the Boiler Makers of Purdue and beat us roundly; Notre Dame was on a roll. In 1950 we went to South Bend to try again. No one was holding out any hope for us against Leahy's powerhouse. They hadn't lost a game in four years and were looking forward to victory number forty.

Our quarterback was only a sophomore, Dale Samuels, a wonderful young man I much admired (and would name a son after). Dale put on an aerial show against the Irish that was unprecedented. "Fan right trailer," I phoned down from the press box where I was perched. Dale rolled right; the right flanker sped downfield; the tight end raced at the safety and shot past his inside shoulder to turn him away from the right halfback, Neal Schmidt, who was barreling toward the goal line between him and the flanker. Dale's pass was perfect. Four times he threw for touchdowns and Notre Dame went down to defeat, their string of victories broken. That year we were besieged with speaking invitations and I spent a lot of the off-season enjoying my roving ambassador's role thoroughly.

Recruiting was something else I liked a lot—traveling around, talking to young players, selling them on Purdue, and competing with other schools for their talents. I especially remember a spectacular quarterback Woody Hayes had his eye on for Ohio State. I told the youngster our brand of football favored his skills, which was true. Also, unlike Woody, we wouldn't object at all to his participating in other sports besides football. I was, in fact, the baseball coach in addition to being the football team's backfield coach, so there would be no problem at all; and the same went for basketball.

Leonard Dawson was the boy's name, from Alliance, Ohio, and he looked good, but he was reserved and fastidious. Still, his poise under pressure was impressive, and he delivered. I liked him a lot, and we got him.

It was obvious he would start his sophomore year, but we wanted to bring him along steadily and not rush him with a premature debut. Why we thought he might be nervous at the prospect of starting at quarterback I'll never know, because Lenny Dawson was the coolest and calmest young man any of us had ever encountered.

Our first opponent was Don Faurot's Missouri Tigers, heavily favored because they'd trounced us the year before. In the dressing room just prior to the game, Head Coach Holcomb gathered the team for some final sober words. Everyone was there, of course, except Leonard.

Collaring me, Coach Holcomb rasped, "Where in the hell is Dawson? Get him in here right away."

I searched the dressing area and training rooms and found him in the john. He was carefully putting on his black jersey so as not to muss his perfectly coifed hair.

"Lenny! Get out here. Stu is ready to talk to the team. Come on!"

"Okay, Coach," he said, while checking himself out in the mirror. "I'll be right there."

He neatly tucked his jersey into his gold pants, took out a comb, and aligned every hair. You'd have thought he was going to the prom. Finally he came out and joined his teammates. After Stu's little talk, as everyone lined up to jog out onto the field for the kickoff, one of the coaches said to him, "Leonard, good luck in your first collegiate game."

Lenny looked puzzled. Very matter-of-factly, he said, "You don't need luck. All you need is ability." He didn't say it egotistically; he said it as if it were an objective observation he had made about something.

Halfway through the first quarter, he went in. I was upstairs in the press box. I called, "Fan right hook," a play we used a lot. The tight end, Johnny Kerr, headed downfield behind the roll, then stopped in an open area. Lenny was rolling right in a moving pocket. The pass went up, quick and precise. Bang. A completion, and the beginning of a record-breaking career, as he threw four touchdown passes that day. Final score: 33 to zip.

Everyone was elated, although we well knew the next week's encounter would be very difficult against Notre Dame. It's hard to exaggerate how powerful Leahy's teams were. Many schools were refusing to face the Fighting Irish. Our only edge was that we were going to take them on in South Bend, their home turf. For some reason we always did better on their home field and had gained some local notoriety as the "Spoiler Makers" of Purdue.

As head coach of the baseball team, over the course of many springs and summers I had taken our boys to Notre Dame for games and had the opportunity to study closely Frank Leahy's methodical training. He was a great coach and he had the finest players.

When we got there, the campus was a madhouse of rabid fans. Everyone on the Purdue squad was very tense in anticipation of the shellacking we were facing, except for Leonard. Completely self-possessed and undaunted by the hostile bedlam enveloping him, he just let fly and did what he'd done the previous week. He threw another four touchdowns, and Purdue beat the invincible Irish, 26–14. By the end of that afternoon there wasn't a reporter or fan in the country who didn't know the young marksman from Alliance, Ohio. Lenny Dawson was a national hero.

The next season, Stu Holcomb got a call from Red Blaik at West Point. Army was going to be facing Notre Dame, and Colonel Blaik wanted to send one of his assistant coaches out to us in West Lafayette to spend some time talking offense with one of the Purdue assistants. I was nominated, Stu informed me.

Stu Holcomb was notoriously bad on remembering names. Even his own children's eluded him at times, and he fumbled with the name of the junior coach who was coming.

"Oh, it's a funny name," he said, squinting as if to picture it better. "Wait a minute. The band leader who has the boat—"

"Guy Lombardo," I said.

"Yeah," Stu said. "That's it, that's it."

Army had a quarterback named Lombardo, so I assumed that's who they were sending. When I was informed the man from West Point had arrived, I expected to see a strapping cadet officer in uniform. Instead, there was a stocky fellow wearing glasses. His face had an Oriental cast, the effect heightened by a wide space between his two front teeth. He looked like Tojo.

"Hank," Stu said, "this is Coach Lombardo."

"It's *Lombardi!*" the guy shouted. "Lombardi, Lombardi. *Not* Lombardo. *Lombardi!*"

"Right," I said, and took him away to an upstairs conference

31

room. Using a blackboard, I attempted to describe our passing game. To my utter surprise, he had no more interest in it than the man in the moon. All he wanted to talk about was running strategies. He had a revolutionary scheme, he said.

"From a full-house backfield, all three backs go to the same side. All three attack to the left, or to the right. The halfback dives, the fullback goes off tackle, and the remaining back goes to the outside." He beamed his odd smile at me. "Nobody will know ahead of time who is to get the ball." This to enhance the faking by the backs.

Running, that's all he wanted to talk about. I had a hell of a time trying to wedge in my explanation of how we had beaten Notre Dame with our passing game. He would wrest the chalk back from me and resume his passionate diatribe on the nuances of his revolutionary sweep. I took back the chalk and tried expounding on the pass. It was like a Marx Brothers comedy. We went back and forth like that all day. By the time I saw Vince Lombardi off on the train back to the United States Military Academy, I was exhausted.

Slumped in Stu's office, I said, "That man has got a head like a brick wall."

I had liked him, though. It was hard not to. The guy almost insisted on it in a way; he was so obstinate and determined.

The next year, as I began my ninth season at Purdue, Vince Lombardi resigned his West Point job. He had signed on as an assistant coach with a pro team, the New York Giants. Gee, I thought, how can a guy interested only in running schemes help a professional team?

After four years at Purdue, my salary topped six thousand dollars, and I finally saved up enough to buy a house. So Phyllis and I decided to get married: just a tiny ceremony, seven o'clock in the morning at St. Mary's Cathedral with only immediate family and Joe and Gail Rudolph as witnesses. For our honeymoon we drove to Chicago for the weekend, forgetting the suitcase with Phyllis's trousseau in the excitement. We went to two football games, the Kelly Bowl game at Soldier's Field and Los Angeles against the Bears. We also took in the Ice Follies. Then it was back to West Lafayette and work.

Coaching Lenny Dawson in his varsity years was pure pleasure most of the time. For three years running, he led the Big Ten in passing and total offense. I even liked his penchant for neatness. Leonard hated to get his uniform soiled and rarely did. On rainy days all the players would look like mud pies, except for Leonard.

In 1955, his junior year, things suddenly changed. In our final team scrimmage, Lenny—who was also our punter and kicker—kicked off. Running down to cover the ball, he got so involved in watching its trajectory that he didn't notice an oncoming blocker until nearly the last second. He put his hands down late to ward off the hit and got his thumb caught in the other guy's shoulder pads. A bone cracked in his thumb. As luck would have it, it was his throwing hand.

We continued to win, even though Lenny's performance was impaired from then on. The season was successful but wobbly. Then, Stu Holcomb took the athletic director's job at Northwestern University.

Although he recommended me as his successor, he and Red Mackey, the athletic director, weren't all that fond of one another and the recommendation was ignored. I didn't get the job. The man who did was Jack Mollenkopf.

I loved Purdue. I had dreamed of being head coach of my alma mater. But I was odd man out. After twelve years, I would have to leave, and Phyllis would have to say good-bye to her hometown. Still, I felt things would work out.

Stu Holcomb recommended me to Red Blaik at West Point, and I went east to meet with him. I also went down to Dallas to talk to Matty Bell, the athletic director of Southern Methodist University. I accepted the job as offensive coach at SMU and went right to work.

Our first opponent of the 1956 season? Who else—Notre Dame. Worse yet, the quarterback was Paul Hornung, one of the best college backs ever. With a record of two wins and eight losses the previous year, SMU was the unanimous underdog going in. Good to their word, Matty Bell and Woody Woodward gave me complete control of the offense, and we prepared some surprises for the warriors from South Bend.

The Mustangs of SMU upset the Irish 19–13 (though not before Paul Hornung audibled a punt into a run and scored a touchdown to bring them within six points). After we left the field, the players cornered me in the locker room and handed me a football. It took me some seconds to realize they had given me the game ball.

That win inspired the squad and we had a successful season, yet afterward Head Coach Woodward resigned. The top spot was suddenly open. Matty Bell wanted me to be the successor, but there was a hitch.

"I've got to be honest with you. The problem is your being a Catholic. I don't know whether Southern Methodist is ready for a Catholic head coach."

The search for a new coach began. A lot of people were rooting for me; the players even submitted a petition on my behalf, but the decision was not forthcoming. The Saturday before the final selection was to be made, Sleepy Morgan, the school's beloved freshman coach, called me. He said he had an unusual proposition to make to me and couldn't do it on the phone. He invited me over.

When I got to his house, he said, "Coach, I told Matty Bell in advance what you were going to say, but I want to tell you anyhow and ask you. Matty Bell would like you to be head coach at SMU, but he says he can't do it because you're Catholic. He's wanted me to ask you if you'd go for his making *me* head coach in name only and your actually running the team."

Herman Morgan was one of the kindest guys in the universe. "Sleepy," I said, "no way."

"Well, I knew you were going to say that, but we thought we'd give it a try anyway, as a last resort. It's the only chance we had to keep you here."

If I was acceptable as a Catholic assistant coach, why wasn't I acceptable as a head coach who was Catholic? I was so embittered I decided to chuck coaching. Who needed this—an athletic department passing you over because you ate fish on Fridays.

I was sulking around the house and unhappy. So I picked up the phone and accepted a long-standing offer with Riddell Sporting Goods Company in Chicago. Then Terry Brennan, head coach of the Fighting Irish, called. He invited me to South Bend to discuss a possible job at Notre Dame. They had just had the worst season in the school's history, winning only two games, and Jim Finks, the backfield coach, left for Canada.

"Gee," Phyllis said, "I hope you don't take that job."

"Don't worry, babe," I said. "I'm not going to." Hank Stram was out of the coaching game. No more low pay and insecurity, long hours and ingratitude.

Terry Brennan received me warmly and started to show me around the beautiful campus and the athletic facilities. I saw the team's gold helmets and the golden dome, and within five minutes I had accepted the post. The mystique had gotten to me as it had to so many others.

Fathers Hesburg and Joyce had de-emphasized the football program because of criticism of the school's becoming a football factory. The policy had proven more effective than desired. I didn't care. Notre Dame had a winning tradition that could overcome gravity.

I knew I had made the right decision when I saw the first school on the upcoming schedule: Purdue!

Game one—my alma mater led by the coach who had helped ease me out of the job he now occupied. I wanted this one bad, and I talked Terry Brennan into doing some skunking: secretly scouting the opposition.

Phyllis's dad ran the Piggly Wiggly store across the street from Purdue's practice field. Our scout was put up on the roof with a bucket of tar and some overalls so he could pretend to be working while spying on the practice sessions under way across the street.

Back in South Bend, I also prevailed upon Terry to befuddle our opposition, as they were undoubtedly skunking us as well. Knowing that a particular sportswriter whose loyalty to Purdue was unequivocal was going to watch us practice, I scrapped the multiple formations I'd been using and put our quarterback, George Izo, in a single-wing formation and had him run plays from it. If things worked as I hoped, word would reach Purdue about our configurations, and they would shift their attention to training against a single-wing instead of our multiple formations.

Back came word from our skunker that Purdue was suddenly working against a single-wing, and I knew we had them. I am not ashamed to say that beating Purdue that next weekend was one of the sweetest wins of my life. Rarely have I enjoyed a victory quite so much. Losing is miserable and winning is fun, but there is nothing that will put a spring in your step quite like well-deserved vengeance.

The team turned around over the course of the new season behind the quarterbacking of George Izo and Bobby Williams, and the play of All-American guard Al Ecuyer, Monty Stickles, Nick Pietrosanti, and Dick Lynch. We finished with a very respectable seven wins, three losses—quite a difference over the previous year.

The second season was nearly as good—6 and 4—and included two heartbreaking losses to Pittsburgh and Army. Still, we were more than satisfied with our progress. The Sunday before Christmas week, I came home from mass and found a phone message from Terry Brennan. He sounded unusual, Phyllis said. I called back. We had all been fired, he told me.

It seemed incredible, if not unreasonable, to let so fine a head coach go after he had delivered back-to-back winning seasons. In fact, in his five-year tenure, Terry had compiled an outstanding record of 32 wins against 18 losses: four winning seasons (8–2, 9–1, 2–8, 7–3, 6–4). I figured there would be repercussions in the press and a long-term negative effect on the school's football, from which it would take a while to recover. Yet, mistake or no, we were out.

What a rat race, I thought. This is ridiculous. Once again I gave serious consideration to chucking it, but Andy Gustafson of the University of Miami collared me at a convention in Cincinnati. They had had a bad season. Let me guess, I thought, and sure enough—2 and 8. The team was in a bind and open to anything, by way of offensive changes, that might help them.

I took the job and went home to break the news to Phyllis. Three jobs in three years; three relocations of households and disruptions of our three sons' lives. We were turning into gypsies. After eight sheltered years at Purdue, I was beginning to see just how dog-eat-dog the profession really was. I thought back to those peaceful seasons under Stu Holcomb, dreaming up new formations, testing new pass patterns, worrying about winning and not much else. Now we were like nomads, and winning was survival.

But you couldn't feel sorry for yourself because nobody made you be a coach. Nobody made you do it. Sure, when bad things happened to people, you felt for the guys involved—yourself included—but you knew it went with the job, and you got on with it. Around one of these corners I knew I would find what I was looking for.

FOUR

FRAN Curci was a terrific quarterback to work with; the squad rallied behind him and started winning. I was enjoying the success of the Miami team and the wonderful weather. The heat just baked the anxiety out of my midwestern bones. At the end of the season, I found myself with speaking engagements scheduled for two consecutive nights: the first in Gary at my old high school, the second in Chicago the following evening.

During the banquet in Gary, a waiter whispered to me that I had a long-distance call from Texas holding on the phone in the kitchen. When I picked up the receiver, there was a familiar voice on the other end asking me to come to Dallas in the morning. It was Lamar Hunt.

He said, "There's a flight leaving Chicago at ten o'clock, gets here at noon. Another leaves at two and gets you back to Chicago in a hurry."

"I'll be there tomorrow," I said. The next morning I flew out, pondering what might await me in Dallas.

The Hunts of Texas were synonymous with oil and money. H. L. Hunt, father of Lamar, Bunker, and Herbert, had amassed a fortune estimated at $600 million and had passed many millions on to his sons to develop further. They invested in many things: precious metals, chemicals, and the like. But what the

sons, especially Lamar, were most interested in was pro foot-
ball. Despite the failure, eight years earlier, of the All-America
Conference (which had fielded teams like the Miami Seahawks,
Chicago Rockets, Los Angeles Dons, New York Yankees, and
Branch Rickey's football Dodgers in Brooklyn), twenty-six-year-
old, six-foot, 175-pound former SMU third-string end Lamar
Hunt was forming an eight-team league to challenge the pow-
erful and well-entrenched NFL.

There were, after all, only fourteen pro teams in the entire
country. Certainly more could be supported and enjoyed by fans
in urban areas that didn't as yet have clubs in their vicinities,
and in major cities large enough to support additional clubs from
a new, rival league. Only a few teams of the All-America Conference had survived its demise: the Cleveland Browns and the
San Francisco 49ers. Most others had been plowed under by
the relentless competition of the NFL. Nonetheless, Lamar Hunt
was undaunted.

The new league would be called the American Football
League. War Hero Joe Foss had been named commissioner and
would be headquartered in Dallas, along with the newly elected
president, Lamar Hunt.

I had heard a lot about this the previous spring, when he'd
approached me after a practice at Miami. Lamar said he'd first
met me at SMU, his much beloved alma mater, after the upset
win against Notre Dame. He had heard about me from his old
college pals, as well as guys like Buzz Kemble and Charley
Arnold, who had been on that SMU team when I was coaching
the offense.

Lamar invited me out to dinner after practice, and over a
wonderful meal he expounded on his ambitious plans. When
the check arrived, he reached in his pockets and came up empty.
Would I mind paying, he asked. Not at all, I said. There I was,
taking a Texas multimillionaire to dinner.

Afterward he wanted to meet my wife and family, and I
obliged. I introduced him to Hank junior, Dale (named for Dale
Samuels), Stu (named for Stu Holcomb), and Phyllis, who was
carrying our fourth child. Lamar was extremely solicitous and

polite. He seemed a genteel and charming young fellow. When he put his feet up as we talked, Phyllis and I exchanged smiles. Lamar Hunt, one of the wealthiest men in the country, had holes the size of silver dollars in both his shoes.

That was the last I'd heard from him until the telephone call. Now I was on my way to meet him in Dallas. We landed on time, which meant I had four hours before my return flight, and I took a cab to his office. An hour after arriving, I was still waiting to see him. When I finally did get in there, what do we talk about? The Notre Dame upset, naturally. The clock was running, and I was getting increasingly concerned.

"Mr. Hunt, I've got to catch that plane at four. Excuse me, but why did you have me come down? What's this about, a coaching job with the new team you're setting up here in Dallas?"

"I guess you could say that," Lamar answered.

I waited, but he didn't volunteer anything more.

"Well, what about the job?"

"Ah, I . . . we—we'd like you to be the head football coach."

I couldn't help myself; I was very excited, though I was sure it didn't show. Head coach! Undoubtedly a lot of people wouldn't have considered it. The NFL had buried the All-America Conference in less than three seasons of head-on competition. This AFL was going to be just as warmly received. However, after my recent sampling of job security in the college ranks, I didn't much care. This twenty-six-year-old entrepreneur had single-handedly launched a serious challenge to the old guard of pro football and organized an impressive little cartel to help mount it.

We talked and talked, and by the time we were through, I had to get to the airport promptly.

"Tell you what," Lamar Hunt said. "I've got a couple more calls to make. Why don't you get my car? It's in a lot about six blocks away. Only exercise I get—walking over. Oh, well. Go there, why don't you, and pick it up. I'll meet you out front and drive you to the airport."

I hiked over to his parking lot and asked for his limousine, expecting a Cadillac I suppose, or a Mercedes, or maybe even a Rolls. The attendant drove up in a four-year-old Oldsmobile that looked like it had crossed a minefield. It was dirty, rusted-out in spots, and the front seat had a terrible hole in it, crudely covered with a threadbare blanket. It was the wrong car, I insisted. Had to be.

"No sir," the attendant said. "It's Mr. Lamar Hunt's automobile all right. I know. I've been trying to buy the sucker from him for six hundred dollars. He wants eight and won't take less. We've been haggling for weeks."

By now it was getting critically late, so I jumped in the rattletrap and drove back toward Lamar's office. Halfway there the engine died. No gas.

I got a push to a filling station and filled it up. Something told me to check the oil. The dipstick was dry. Zero. No oil whatsoever. I filled it with several quarts of oil and raced over to Lamar's building. He was waiting, I was relieved to see, as I pulled up. When he got in, I told him the story of his car, and he laughed like hell as we drove.

We all waste a lot of time and money, he told me. Organization of time was of utmost importance.

I blazed my best smile at him and glanced at my watch. Eighteen minutes to make the plane. Lamar, meanwhile, expanded on his philosophy as we sped along. Investments of one's time or money in things that yielded no possible return were much to his disliking.

"Like shoes," he said. "No return there whatsoever. Hate putting money in shoes."

Or gas and oil, I thought.

I made my flight by a whisker, and only when the plane had taken off did I realize that I'd neither accepted the job formally nor come to terms. So we wound up negotiating my contract by phone. In eleven years of college coaching, I had progressed from a starting salary of $3,600 to a formidable $7,500. What the hell, I decided. Lamar's father was making $200,000 a day, and this was the big leagues—pro ball. I held out for $20,000 and got it! Then I flew back down to Dallas for the announcements. The press response to the news of my appointment was nearly universal: *Hank who?*

I returned home to help pack up the family yet again, and returned to Dallas ahead of them to look for housing. Phyllis was to follow with the kids. On Good Friday I drove out to pick them up at the train station. It was hot. The train had stopped a half-mile out for some reason, and there was my poor wife, hiking down the tracks carrying two of the boys, and my mother lugging Stu and Baby Julie. So, like migrant farmworkers we came to Dallas. I was determined we weren't going to be moving again anytime soon. This team, whatever it was going to be called, was going to succeed.

I was head coach at the age of thirty-four. So what if there was no team yet, no name, no uniforms, no team colors or insignia, no footballs, helmets, players? We were all starting out new—the Titans in New York, the Bills, Patriots, Broncos, Oilers, Chargers, Raiders. It was new and exciting, and I loved it.

I hired three coaches, really good ones: Bill Walsh for offense, an ex-Steeler and Notre Dame lineman; Tom Catlin, who had just retired from the Cleveland Browns and had been an All-American at Oklahoma, as the defensive-line coach (a pilot during the war, he was a solid guy and an outstanding teacher); and to coach the defensive backs, I signed Ed Hughes, a former Tulsa star and a terrific defensive back with Tom Landry on the Giants. I got Wayne Rudy as trainer and Bobby Yarborough for equipment.

The team name was decided by Lamar—the Dallas Texans. Eight years earlier, the NFL had tried to launch a team in Dallas with that same name, and it had failed. Lamar called on their former owner, Giles Miller, and got his permission to use the name. Lamar deliberately revived it as if to show the National Football League how it should be done. It was like a gauntlet.

It didn't take the NFL long to rise to the challenge. They'd earlier reversed themselves and granted a new NFL franchise in Dallas—the Cowboys. They were going head on at the flagship team owned by the president of the new league in the city that was the AFL's headquarters. And all over the country, accusations and lawsuits flew like footballs as the vying sets of owners went at it.

It didn't help matters that the Cowboys' new head coach was to be Tom Landry, former assistant coach with the New York Giants and an ex-Longhorn star from the University of Texas. It didn't help either that their general manager was named Tex Schramm (he had been *christened* Texas). It made us all the more disposed to the idea of signing as many Southerners and Texans as possible.

Regardless of what you read about the drafting of players, many are already spoken for before a collegiate season ends, months before an actual league draft. Free agents and over-looked college talent were what we had to scrutinize, even as we tried to sign the big collegiate names that might influence others to try the AFL.

At 185 pounds, Walt Corey was not what we were looking for, but he had the kind of heart and intelligence that we badly needed, and I signed him as a free agent, frankly expecting him to last only a season or two given his lack of size. The same was true of Smokey Stover. He had the same problem but a lot of talent, and we signed him too, with similarly pessimistic ex-pectations about his longevity. Well, they both took up weight training on their own and steadily increased their weight and durability. (Over the years their weight rose from 185 pounds to 240.) Their intensity and their play were an inspiration.

We signed Ray Collins, who'd played with the Giants; Paul Miller, an ex-Ram; Marvin Terrell from Ole Miss; Jon Gilliam from the Packers; Johnny Bookman from Miami; Ed Bernet from the Steelers. The big break was general manager Don Rossi's signing Chris Burford of Stanford. That really opened the door for other blue-chip players to join the Texans and even the AFL—Abner Haynes, an amazing back from North Texas State; quarterbacks Cotton Davidson from Baylor and Fran Curci from Miami; Johnny Robinson from LSU; and Jack Spikes and Sherrill Headrick from Texas Christian. The team was coming together—on paper, anyway.

We took a lame shot at getting Don Meredith and missed; he

went to the Cowboys. And I actually passed on Jim Otto because of worries about the injuries that were plaguing him even in college. (Otto is ensconced in the Hall of Fame.) We did get Jerry Cornelison, the right tackle from SMU; left tackle Charlie Diamond; Carroll Zarruba, the Nebraska running back whom we converted to a corner; Jim Swink of TCU; Duane Wood from Oklahoma State; Dave Grayson; Curley Johnson; Paul Rochester. The roster was filling up.

At Lamar's house we piled up the living room with all sorts of football gear sent in by manufacturers, from which we selected the equipment we wanted. Using Don Rossi as a mannequin, we tried it all on right there. The colors were next. We decided on white, red, and gold: white pants with red and gold trim, a bright red jersey with white numbers and gold trim and a number on the sleeve, and red helmets bearing the silhouette of the sovereign state of Texas with a gold star thrown in for Dallas.

A practice field was next. The local professional baseball park was grabbed off by the Cowboys, so we had to build our own. Lamar was very fond of SMU, and we leased a site immediately across from the campus. He had owned and operated a batting-cage gallery on that lot while still an undergraduate and had a strong attachment to the place.

I spent a lot of time putting together playbooks, getting organized, and talking over our approach. Finally, we headed for training camp, which for reasons I couldn't understand was in Roswell, New Mexico. Why leave the state—never mind the city—you were going to play in? It wasn't like we were a baseball team. But the plans had been made far in advance. Besides, said Charley Burton, the sports editor of *The Dallas Morning News,* all the fun was in leaving town and going away somewhere where you could have a lot of stag parties and incidents.

New Mexico was beautiful but hot, and infested with large mosquitoes. They were big and plentiful. We lived in dorms that had no air conditioning and we were forced to keep open the windows, which had no screens, so those mangy bugs did everything but carry us off. What with the heat and these pests, jumping into one of the irrigation ditches surrounding the field became the thing to do after each practice. Deflating the tires on my coaching tower was the other favorite sport.

Every single day we worked on fundamentals: blocking, tackling, line takeoffs, punt protection, pass protection, place-kicking, kick-blocking, bag drills, play execution, and even fumble recovery. For at least five minutes, all the linemen and backs drilled at just falling on the ball. They all thought this was kind of crazy at their level, but saw that it paid off to be confident about handling every contingency. The quarterbacks, likewise, were constantly drilling—running in circles about fifteen yards around, throwing first from the right, then from the left, as they jogged. They also threw at a tire suspended by a rope, a drill familiar to most amateur players, except that this tire was in constant motion. To get these passers prepared for some of our taller friends in the league, I had an obstacle built that was about six feet high, over which they had to throw. It had extensions on the sides to approximate pursuers on rollouts.

I wanted nothing left to chance. All games involve repetition, so you have to get your people to do things precisely and consistently. Football, I tried to convince them, is about seconds—four, five, six at most—during which they have to give everything they've got. "You have to dance every dance," I told them.

They did. The practice sessions were tough. What with the heat, the physical contact, and the tension of competing for berths, fights would break out. Nothing serious; the guys were just intense and involved. I kept two pairs of heavy sixteen-ounce boxing gloves in the football bag, and every time a fight occurred, we would stop everything and form a circle around the two disputants. They would box with those heavy gloves for as long as it took to get it out of their systems. If things were kind of dull and slow, in fact, I would get one of the players to pick a fight just to liven everyone up.

We had a lot of white Southerners on the team, and a lot of black Southerners. Neither group had had much exposure to

45

the other before joining the Texans; most had played their college ball at segregated schools. It didn't make any difference, I told them, whether they were black, white, or polka-dotted. We just wanted winners.

At first they wouldn't even drink out of the same water buckets on the field. But after a week of banging on one another in 103-degree heat, they were drinking from the same buckets and the same dippers. It was a small sign of something much bigger about them as individuals and as a group. They were changing, learning respect for each other, and becoming a team.

Meanwhile, we took their measure as players. Back in my first year of coaching, I had met an assistant coach from Princeton named John Steigman who was into computers, which were then unknown. He was a mathematician, and he introduced me to measuring player performance as objectively as possible. So for years I recorded every player's output in practice, and I could tell you how many completions a quarterback had thrown on any given day, what percentage of field goals a kicker had made from a particular section of the field, how many times each ball carrier had run, how many passes a receiver had caught or dropped, and how well or badly each had been thrown. The results were translated into percentages that gauged each team member's performance. The record also told us how thorough the training was and helped the coaches make sure everyone performed a proper number of repetitions. It was partly a checklist and partly a kind of batting average.

In addition to training the troops, promotion was another of my duties as head coach. The rivalry of the two hometown clubs was creating a lot of competition for fans. Everything imaginable was done to sell tickets: a Friend of the Policeman Day, Barbers' Day, a Grocery Bowl, a Huddle Club for kids which basically let them in for free. One fan suggested a showdown between the Texans and the Cowboys, a one-game shoot-out to decide which team would get out of town.

Lamar came up with the idea of buying thirty imported cars and getting thirty young belles to drive around the city selling tickets to companies and organizations. They wore cowgirl outfits, and the resourceful lady who sold the most tickets was going to get her car as a bonus. Lamar asked me to address them on the subject of the Texans and the manly art of football. It was such a success that I was prevailed upon to work my magic on a larger gathering of potential female fans. Anything for the cause.

I appeared before a group of two hundred women, the only guy in the room. As I didn't have a clue as to how much they might know about the sport, I chose to err on the side of caution. Referring to the blackboard I had marked off to represent the 5-yard strips and 1-yard hash marks, I began.

"This is a football field. . . ."

After listening to my discourse, one woman raised her hand and posed her question: "Y'all are explainin' this right well, but I'd like to know why the referee steps off penalties if those little ol' hash lines already divide up the field by single yards."

"He steps off penalties to keep busy," I said, quite candidly.

"Thank you," she said.

I smiled and nodded. This wasn't so difficult. I picked up my next prop. "This," I said, "is a football helmet," and I launched into my lecture on the helmet. There was only one question afterward.

"With all those bars, how is it quarterbacks get their noses broken?"

"Because the linebackers are very accurate," I said, and took up the next demonstration item. "This," I said, "is a football."

After listening to my explanation of its uses and abuses, a woman waved at me from the back and half stood.

"Is it improper to kick the ball too far?" she said.

I smiled. "No."

"Coach Stram," said a lady sitting down front, "why don't y'all ever punt the ball through the goalposts and get three points."

"Because," I said, "it's against the rules."

FIVE

IF you had seen one National Football League team, you had seen them all. Because in the sixties, you understand, the NFL was absolutely dominated by the New York Giants. Whatever the Giants did was gospel, like the two-formation offense, and the 4-3 defense with man-to-man pass coverage. Deviation from these norms was frowned upon.

The man inadvertently responsible for this dogma was Giants Head Coach Jim Lee Howell. His approach was extremely successful and much respected. Those assistant coaches who had worked under his tutelage eventually left and fanned out through the league, carrying his systems with them like disciples. So did players who took up coaching upon retiring. There were Vince Lombardi and Tom Landry in the first generation, followed by their protégés, such as Tom Fears, Norb Hecker, Allie Sherman, and so on down the line. They had played and coached Jim Lee Howell's system and believed in it because it had worked.

It even reached into the new AFL, in the persons of Sid Gillman, who had learned his trade with the LA Rams; Lou Rymkus, who had played for the Browns and coached for the Packers and now brought the Word to the Houston Oilers; and Buster Ramsey, former defensive coordinator with the Lions, newly appointed head coach of the Buffalo Bills. They molded their new teams in the image of the NFL ideal, the Giants.

There were exceptions, to be sure, like ex-Giant Tom Landry's innovative offenses; but he was an NFL purist when it came to defense. The basic credo was run the ball, and if you get in trouble, throw. Football was a running game of hard knocks; the idea was to grind out the yardage and wear down the other guy. The NFL's teams all looked like one another because their coaches had all gone to the same school: You run and pass from the pro set, defend with a 4-3, and cover receivers one-on-one.

Not so in the American Football League. For one thing, few of the coaches in the AFL had experience in the pros. Most had been coaching college teams when they were tapped to head the newly founded clubs. They had their own various notions and weren't particularly impressed with the idea of copying the rival league's model of how things were to be done.

We weren't out to revolutionize anything. Football coaches are, by necessity, pragmatists first. We were simply solving a practical set of problems by relying mainly on the basic methods we had developed and used in our previous posts. Everything we did was predicated on only one thing: Will it help us win? If we thought "yes," we didn't care what anybody else said. We were going to do it. In some ways, it was the biggest lesson I learned—simply to stick to my guns and stay with what I believed would work for us.

Few of the coaches in the AFL bought the conventional wisdom of the NFL. The league was typified by guys like Eddie Erdelatz, the nationally known head coach of the Naval Academy for eight years who had made Navy absolutely formidable. He was the Oakland Raiders' coach and very much his own man when it came to style and a team's personality. Also Sammy Baugh. Although he had been a quarterback on the NFL's Redskins, he had always favored a passing offense. Hell, he loved it, and he coached it at the tiny Texas university of Hardin-Simmons, giving the school a success and reputation in football far out of proportion to its size. Baugh would be named head coach of the New York Titans.

Sid Gillman, who loved the passing game too, became coach

of the Los Angeles Chargers; Frankie Filchock, from the Canadian League, took over the Broncos; and Lou Saban was named coach of the Patriots.

Coaching is teaching, as the old saying goes, and you can't teach anything with confidence unless you know it inside out. Like many of my peers in the AFL, I just felt more comfortable and confident teaching what I had developed and tested in college. I favored a variety of formations over the mere two used in the NFL, and I like to use a lot of motion on offense. Also, I didn't think much of the 4-3 defense, with its four down linemen and three linebackers. I preferred a lot of odd spacing, with a man on the nose of the opposing center. This 3-4 defense or a 5-3 alignment were much more familiar to the AFL people. There were none of the prejudices among us about their being amateurish or substandard—unprofessional. We incorporated what we knew and taught it, well. Besides, the majority of our players were very young, recently out of college, and a lot more familiar with an entirely different brand of football from that being played in the NFL.

I never understood why everybody in pro ball insisted that players fresh out of college adapt themselves to something completely different from what they had known since high school. It was like asking every new player to play a new position. It put a tremendous strain on them, mentally and physically, as they struggled to overcome their conditioned instincts to fit in with the pro systems. I thought they could adapt a lot faster and easier to a style of defensive and offensive play closer to what they'd known for so many years, like the 3-4 or Oklahoma defense with odd spacing, and rollout passing. Besides, we had more talent at linebacker than on the defensive line, so it made more sense. Little did I know it would be taken so badly by our neighbors in the NFL, or that this criticism would go on for years as we introduced man-in-motion plays, a tight-I formation, double tight ends, a moving pocket, and stack defenses.

I got a live, in-person taste of things to come that first summer of the AFL's inaugural year, 1960. Just before the preseason I was invited to a clinic in Lubbock, Texas, to give a little talk. Tom Landry preceded me. He elaborated on the virtues of the 4-3 defense and man-for-man coverage: right out of the New York Giants' catechism.

I talked about zone coverage and the rollout pass I had coached at SMU, Notre Dame, the University of Miami, and Purdue. Against a zone defense, I explained, an offense had to travel a lot slower. Anytime you were in a man-for-man mode, you invited the possibility of a big play. Sure, you might get the quarterback before he uncorked the ball, but if you didn't, the odds were excellent that he would hurt you with a long yardage pass. I didn't want that quarterback to be able to strike in an instant. I wanted the opposition to travel slowly, and I wanted to eliminate the quick touchdown. If they were forced to run ten or fifteen plays in their drive, why, in all probability they might stop themselves, or we might just wear them down. The odds were better for their making mistakes. The odds favored zone coverage over the NFL's pet, man-for-man coverage.

After the talks, we went over to Detroit quarterback Bobby Layne's house to socialize. Landry and I were standing at the edge of the crowd, and I said to him: "Tom, I can't understand why somewhere during a game a pro-football team hasn't used a zone defense. I've been a lifelong fan of the Bears, for instance—and of the Cardinals when they were in Chicago—and I've seen them have a game won on numerous occasions only to wind up losing on a pass thrown to somebody who looked like he ran out of the bleachers, he was so uncovered. They would have everyone blitzing and nobody on the receiver in their man-for-man scheme, and they'd lose. For years I've wondered why it is that the NFL doesn't employ a zone."

Landry shook his head. "In the National Football League you cannot use zone defense successfully."

"Why?"

"Well," he said, "the quarterbacks in the NFL would cut you to ribbons."

"Yes, but how, Tom?"

51

"They'd just slice you up like fruit."

"Right," I said, and turned to Bobby Layne. "Bobby, as one of the top quarterbacks in the NFL, what would you do if you looked up over your center and saw a zone defense staring back?"

"Oh," he said, "I'd cut it to pieces."

"Right, but how—how would you do it?"

"No way in the world they could work it against me. I'd cut 'em up like a barracuda."

I went back to Dallas, and we began our schedule of exhibition games. I used a 3-4 defense and zone coverage in our game plan, and suddenly I was getting the party line from some of my own staff, particularly Ed Hughes. A terrific coach, he had played for Landry with the Giants and, I realized, felt terribly uncomfortable with zone defenses. Still, I knew I wasn't running a popularity contest. In business you talk in terms of success or failure; in the business of football it's winning or losing. My job was winning, and I just couldn't worry about what the press or the NFL coaches said, or even about the objections of my own assistants. My role was to decide, and I did.

The Texans won their first outing against the Raiders and kept on winning. Ed raised the issue once again: He wanted man-for-man. By the time of our second encounter with the Houston Oilers (we had won the first 27–10), it was getting serious.

I explained the obvious: Yes, quarterback George Blanda was an ex-NFL great and a real threat. It was precisely because of him, and the great receivers he had in Hennigan and Groman—not to mention Billy Cannon and Willard Dewveall—that I wanted our backs *not* to take them on man-for-man.

"Look," I said, "we're going to play a very simple zone. We're going to rotate right and left all the time, and always have a safety man in the hole. If George Blanda beats us, he's going to do it very, very slowly. He's not going to beat us fast, throwing those home runs against man-for-man coverage."

Ed was furious. "There's no way in the world we can play a zone against George Blanda and the Oilers."

"Why?" I said.

"Because he's going to chop us up into little chunks."

"Listen," I said. "We're going to play a zone and hope for the best."

So we squared off in Tulsa and used the zone, intercepted seven passes, and won the game 24–3. Ed was all the more upset, it seemed. You can't win, I thought. The feeling was pervasive in these guys that you had to do it the NFL way or it was somehow illegitimate. (Two years later, in fact, Ed was to quit over this after yet another win featuring the zone.) They were sincerely dedicated to the one way of doing it.

Such rigidity in pro football was not unfamiliar. For years, the single-wing had been devoutly used in the pros until the Chicago Bears destroyed the Washington Redskins 73–0 in the 1940 championship game, prompting a mass defection to the T-formation. I had a hunch something similar was going to befall this latest idol, the NFL system.

That the NFL people believed so fervently was fine, really. The problem was, they couldn't see the possibility of anything else maybe working too, or working against their hallowed formations. Consequently, a condescending attitude toward the AFL grew with the first season's approach, and you could see this was going to go on for years. To be honest, it left few of us in the new league unperturbed. For them to have so little regard for us was irritating, but we knew eventually the reckoning would come. If the AFL teams didn't fold from lack of fans and television revenues, one day we would knock on the door of the National Football League and demand parity. And then the showdown would come where we so badly wanted it—on the field.

We had won all our exhibition games so far, and we went to Little Rock, Arkansas, a week before facing the Denver Broncos there in a preseason matchup. Stupidly, it hadn't occurred to us that we'd have black team members being refused accommodations, but we did. We had to book our players into hotels in another part of the town entirely—not exactly what you want to see happen to a team. Worse yet, the hotels available to blacks were wretched. It was a lousy situation made all the worse by the glaring differences in facilities. But Abner Haynes, Clemon Daniels, David Grayson, and the others were more understanding than anyone had a right to expect. Even so, some of their teammates and coaches were literally in tears over the unfairness and obstinacy, and we actually considered chucking the whole thing and going home. Who needed this? It was only the deportment of the blacks on the team that made the situation tolerable, even for a week. Nonetheless, everyone felt miserable for days.

Meanwhile, I was told Lamar had booked me for seventeen speaking engagements during the week leading up to the game. There was no way I could meet such a schedule of appearances and still do my job, I told Rossi. Lamar was going to be upset by this, Rossi said, and he was.

A telegram arrived: "Please understand that you are being fined $500 for not fulfilling obligations." To cap a perfect week, I thought.

We played the Broncos with a vengeance they no doubt found surprising, and we beat them 46–6 and went home to Dallas. I called up Lamar and drove over to his house. He was in the bedroom, reading and writing notes. I gave him my thoughts on the fine and hit him up for a raise. I guess I made my point. The next day, he rescinded the fine and gave me the raise, which was typical of Lamar. He was basically open and fair.

We took on Houston at home in the Cotton Bowl, in our last exhibition game, and beat them handily, 24–3, in front of fifty thousand fans. Now it was time for the real thing.

After six straight preseason wins, we opened the actual season against the Los Angeles Chargers, coached by Sid Gillman. At the half we led 20–0; the Texans looked good. Lamar Hunt, however, looked dejected in the locker room.

"Boy," he said, "if we win this game in an overwhelming fashion, it's going to hurt the franchise and the television potential in this region."

The owner of the Texans was being the league president for

the moment. "Listen," I said, "don't worry about anybody else's team just now. Worry about your own. Let the commissioner worry about the league; that's his responsibility. Worry about winning."

Well, the Chargers roared back in the second half, hot as pistols. On the final drive of the fourth quarter, the L.A. quarterback and future New York Senator, Jack Kemp, had the ball on his own 7-yard line. He was boxed, I thought. We ought to have the game bagged. No such luck. With the help of four successive penalties, they advanced down the field and scored, beating us 21–20.

One lousy point, but it might as well have been a million. They won; we lost. I sat outside the locker room to cool off where the team wouldn't see me. Getting on people who have just lost is counterproductive, I always thought. I was not the ranting type. A latticed wall separated our side from the visitors' locker-room door. Upset with the loss, I slammed my can of soda against that wall, splattering it all over.

We played the Raiders next and knocked them off 34–16. Then it was on to Dallas for our first home game of the season, our second against the Chargers. We avenged our earlier loss to them by shutting them out, 17–0, with forty-two thousand Texans looking on. So we were 2 and 1 on the season going into New York for game four.

With Al Dorow's great rollout passes and Art Powell's incredible receptions, they beat us 37–35. Two games lost by a total of three points. Life in the big leagues could give you an ulcer in no time.

The next game didn't make me feel any better. We lost to Oakland, 20–19. Maybe I should reexamine my life and aspirations, I thought. Houston at least made things a bit more definite, bashing us by a score of 20–10 in front of their hometown rooters, which put us at a miserable two wins to four losses as we approached midseason. Thankfully, we won our next two games on the road and headed home to face Denver in the Cotton Bowl.

While I kept busy on the field coaching, Lamar took a hand

at welcoming new prospects. We had been lucky in the draft, landing the fearsome center of the Texas Tech squad, E. J. Holub, and besting the Cowboys, who had also had him down as their first choice. Our other acquisitions were similarly impressive: Jerry Mays of SMU; Ohio State's 292-pound tackle, Jim Tyrer; Bob Lilly of TCU; and then No. 2 choice of the Cardinals, end Fred Arbanas.

All five had met at the East-West game in San Francisco and hit it off so well that they vowed to sign with the same team, and did, except for Bob Lilly. A Cowboy scout got hold of him and took him out on the town. Lilly woke up the next morning with six hundred-dollar bills strewn across him and his copy of the nine-thousand-dollar contract he had signed. Jerry Mays was furious and called the Cowboys owner, Clint Murchison. Mr. Murchison thanked the young player for bringing the matter to his attention and said Bob Lilly could tear up the contract. He would fly to San Francisco the following day, and if Lilly were interested, Murchison would personally sign him to a fifteen-thousand-dollar contract, with a five-thousand-dollar bonus thrown in—which is how we lost Bob Lilly to the Cowboys.

Lamar invited the Gargantuan Tyrer and Fred Arbanas to Dallas to see the city and the team they might be joining. He met them at the airport with his father, and Lamar, all of 175 pounds, took Jim Tyrer's carry-on bag while his dad took Arbanas's. Lamar was as excited as a kid at Christmas.

The two collegians looked around for a limo and driver, but the Hunts led them to the parking lot, past a typical Dallas collection of swank automobiles, and on into the cheaper back lot. The foursome stopped at the back of a 1953 Hudson. It was in such sorry shape that Lamar couldn't get the trunk open. Tyrer, known to his intimates at "the Great Pumpkin," grabbed the handle and just about lifted the lid out of the car body. Then they all got into the automobile, and the players began their weekend as guests of the Texans. Well, they fell in love with the city, which was easy to do, and watched us beat Denver 34–7. They signed with the Texans.

We flew to Boston to meet the Patriots at Braves Field on a

Friday night. It was scheduled for Friday evening, so as not to interfere with collegiate schedules or compete directly with the NFL. The morning of the game I went to services at St. Cecilia's. Coming out, I ran into the priest who had officiated.

"Say," he said, "aren't you Hank Stram? I'm Father Mackey."

I shook his hand as he beamed a smile.

"Geez," he exclaimed. "What a surprise. I always thought you were Jewish."

We kidded back and forth for a while and I just instantly knew I liked this man. Impulsively I invited him to the game to sit on the bench with the team, provided it wouldn't compromise him with his Boston parishioners.

"Oh, my," he said. "That would be terrific!"

"Then count on it, Father." I had another thought. "In fact, our pregame meal is at four, and you would be most welcome."

He accepted. I left him with the strong feeling that I had made a friend for life. Well, he was just a great guy. He'd been a track star at Boston College and was very adept at marathon walking. He also had a great sense of humor, and all the players loved him right off.

We played the game at eight that evening, but even with Mackey on the bench, our luck was not good. We lost. So the next morning I was somewhat gray when I went back to St. Cecilias's for early mass.

Mackey was the celebrant. Afterward I stopped to say good-bye. He laughed as I approached.

"You know," he said, "I'm impressed."

"Why?" I asked.

"Because I've seen a lot of coaches at mass before a game, but you're the only one I've seen afterward."

I laughed and said I was getting a head start on next week's competition. Mackey had that rare ability to lift people and lighten their load. It would be another year before we'd be in Boston again, and I would miss him, I realized.

"See you next year," I said, and left.

We got banged up by the New York Titans next. At five wins

57

and six losses, we had ourselves a losing season in the making and three games remaining, all at home. We *had* to redeem ourselves; I had to do something.

I gathered the team together and told them: If we didn't play like I knew we could play, then we'd play for nothing. No pay. It was an outrageous threat, no doubt illegal, and I meant it. Their response was in the finest tradition of paid professional athletes prompted to contemplate the potential state of being unpaid. They chopped up the Oilers 24–0; avenged themselves upon the Patriots, 34–0; and nearly shut out the Broncos, 34–7.

We were 8 and 6 on the year, and we were a team!

SIX

FOUR of our guys were selected for the All-League squad, and halfback Abner Haynes was voted Player of the year. Although he was only 170 pounds, he had racked up 875 yards on the ground—576 in pass receptions and nearly 300 more returning punts. Besides being a sensational receiver, he possessed a wonderful sense of humor. Once, when he was knocked senseless during a game, I rushed out onto the field and knelt over him.

"Where did you get hurt, Abner?" I asked.

"Right here where I'm layin'," he said.

I was relieved to see he was conscious. "That," I said, "is grammatically incorrect. Chickens lay and people lie."

"Sorry, Coach, I'm not lieing. I got hurt right here where I'm laying."

Lamar Hunt lived just down the street from us, and invariably he would call and say to come on over for some hamburgers. His wife, Rosemary, was a terrific cook and fun. We went over often, and Lamar and I would shoot baskets in the back and talk shop. Or else he would call and invite us out to dinner with a group of his Dallas friends at Campisi's, just a little Italian place off the SMU campus. The first time we joined him, with a few other couples, he asked for the bill at the end of the meal, checked the addition, and announced that we should pony up sixteen bucks apiece.

Laughing, I turned to his pal, Buzz Kemble, sitting next to me, and said, "He's kidding."

Buzz shook his head, amused. "He's not. Reach for the hip."

Like the prominently displayed holes in his shoes, or his insistence on flying only coach class, this affectation of middle-class behavior was part of Lamar's disarming and premeditated charm. Whenever the tab for one of our pickup dinners was really serious, Lamar would always pay.

Golf dates were just as spontaneous. Lamar and I would just pile into his car and take off for a course we liked in Fort Worth. I'd still be in my practice clothes, and he would always forget his wallet. So there would be Lamar Hunt, Texas millionaire, at the wheel of his rattletrap car, stopped at the toll booth and writing a check for twenty-five cents to get us through. Horns would be honking behind us, the toll collectors laughing. "Ah, lad," I would say in my best Frank Leahy brogue that Lamar loved. "Would you be needing a pen, Mister Hunt?"

We were quite the odd couple. What with my father having been a custom-made-clothes salesman, I grew up very clothes conscious and over the years accumulated a huge wardrobe: hundreds of sports jackets and suits, and several dozen shoes. Lamar, on the other hand, owned one sports jacket, one suit, and one pair of shoes. Often I would ask him about this. Why, I wanted to know, did he own only the one pair of shoes he had on his feet?

Lamar shrugged. "Because you can only wear a single pair at a time. The rest just sit there in the closet, depreciating."

Also, if one of his two shoes developed a hole, he would have only that one shoe repaired, never both.

"Lamar," I would say, exasperated. "Why didn't you have them both done?"

"Because," he said, looking surprised, "the other shoe didn't need it."

Just before training camp opened, I went up to Green Bay, Wisconsin, to visit Vince Lombardi. Vince was very cordial and took me to dinner at the local country club. The next day,

I talked to his coaches. I watched the team practice and waved to some familiar faces.

It was very obvious that one man was in charge. They all feared him a little and respected him a lot, and he kept them highly disciplined and organized. What he had learned from Red Blaik at West Point was much in evidence. He was a hard taskmaster, tough and demanding, yet a generous and compassionate man at the same time. Running the ball was a religion with him. So was simplicity. He wasn't interested in outsmarting anybody, just in beating them. In fact, he seemed to relish the idea that the opposing team would know exactly what they'd be facing in terms of strategy. It was almost part of the game plan: Here we come, try and stop us. Knowing what the Packers were going to do to you seemed to make it all the worse. The opposing team had no alibi left and would be crushed psychologically as well as physically by Green Bay's power sweeps.

A number of people were surprised that Vince Lombardi would take the time to talk to an unproven young coach from a rival league. They didn't know Lombardi, or about our meeting years earlier. I thanked him for his trouble and hurried back to Dallas, anxious to get on with the '61 season.

To exploit Abner Haynes to the fullest, I put in an I-formation with the help of my former Purdue teammate and friend, John McKay, who was using it at a college on the Coast. Abner ran well from it in practice. Across town, our neighbors, the Cowboys, had logged a terrible season their first year—no wins, eleven losses, and one tie. I felt good going into the regular season. But the feeling was short-lived. We lost our opener in Dallas to the Chargers, won over the Raiders, Oilers, and Broncos, then lost the next six games in a row. Lamar and I were due at a boosters luncheon. He called and said he wanted to see me beforehand.

Walking over from the parking lot, I realized it was the first time he had ever summoned me to his office since I had become head coach, and I began to wonder if this wasn't my last mile. I was a nervous wreck by the time I saw him, but I hid it pretty well even as I waited for the bad news. It never came.

Lamar was as constructive and positive as ever. His one suggestion was about our quarterback, Cotton Davidson. He urged me not to announce who was starting for us until late in the week, in order to keep the pressure off me and Cotton, whom the fans were not adoring at the moment.

Cotton was having a tough year. A year earlier, everyone had thought Fran Curci, whom I had coached at Miami, would be the shoo-in for the job because of our prior relationship. But to me, Cotton seemed the obvious candidate. He was a young guy, just down from the Canadian League; he had played his college ball at Baylor. I had never seen a quarterback throw sideline patterns with such a tight spiral. Davidson could stand on one hash mark, throw patterns down the opposite side of the field, and hit receivers right on the numbers. But in actual games, he was having trouble eluding rushers and getting the ball where he wanted it to go. He was also having terrible luck, as in our last game in Boston.

Behind 28–21, we had the ball on our own 45, with fifty-one seconds left. Cotton threw a pass to Chris Burford, and we were on the Patriots' 11. Boston fans poured down onto the field, even though there was just enough time left for one last play. They barely managed to clear the field, leaving fans wall-to-wall along the sidelines and end zone.

We called time-out and set up a slant pass to Chris. Cotton took the ball from center and fired. It ricocheted off somebody's hand and bounced around the end zone, incomplete. The game was over. Cotton was more than dejected, he seemed unwired, and he kept on insisting that somebody in a khaki jacket had knocked down the pass. I even asked our trainer to check him out, fearing he had suffered a blow to the head or something.

Back in Dallas, we ran the film of the game for the coaches. At the very end, what do we see but a bystander jog across the end zone on the snap and deflect Cotton's make-or-break pass. With all those people surrounding the field, he just blended right in. It was one of the best defensive plays I had seen all year, and I suggested we try to find the guy and sign him as a prospect. It was either that or shoot him.

Our expectations of play-offs and a chance at the championship were over. Everybody knew it, including Vince Lombardi. Vince called and asked for a favor: Would I let him have our place kicker?

I had signed a tough old pro, Ben Agajanian. Lombardi needed someone with experience, someone who had been there, because he was going to be in the NFL play-offs. Ben was a great kicker near the end of his career. There wouldn't be many seasons left for him, or many chances for a championship game. Sure, I said, and sent Agajanian to Vince. It turned out to be the first trade between the National and American leagues, even though it was unofficial. Officially in the eyes of the NFL we didn't exist.

We won three of our last four games, but it was all academic insofar as a title was concerned: Our season record was a miserable 6 and 8. Meanwhile, Green Bay blanked the Giants 37–0 for the NFL title.

The off-season wafted across my days with welcome relief. I went to Pittsburgh to a coaches' convention and looked up a former college player of mine who was with the Cleveland Browns but still living in Pittsburgh after having played three seasons with the Steelers.

It was great to see Lenny Dawson, and we had a happy reunion. But I could tell something was wrong, and I pressed him to talk about it. Lenny, it turned out, was really downcast. In five seasons as a pro, he had thrown a total of twenty-four passes. We discussed this for a long time. If there was any way for him to get out of his contract with the Browns, I said, I'd happily sign him.

When his coach, Paul Brown, called to tie up the details of our picking up Lenny, the conversation was worrisome. Lenny, he said, was not in good shape. His arm was not strong, and he couldn't throw the ball as he had at Purdue, when I'd coached him. His skills, Brown explained, were sadly diminished, and his attitude was poor. He felt he owed me that candid assessment.

I took Leonard anyway, only half believing what I had heard.

63

Lenny Dawson was one of the finest quarterbacks I had ever seen, incredibly cool under fire and accurate. He had led the Big Ten in passing and total offense for three years. I flew to Pittsburgh after an appointment in Buffalo and had him sign the necessary papers and contracts at the airport. Then, confident and full of high hopes, I went back to Dallas and prepared for our upcoming training camp.

Lenny soon arrived and joined the squad. I hadn't bothered to look at any recent film of his rare appearances over the last five years. He had played so little that I fully expected him to be rusty. Anyway, I had recruited him as a college player and knew him as well as any coach could. It made watching him in practice all the more painful. He was hopelessly slow on his feet, and the rotation of his passes was extremely slow. The tight spiral was gone—vanished. Our quarterbacks were normally getting back into the pocket and setting to throw in a second and a half, or less. Lenny barely made it in two. Five years of warming the bench on the sidelines had really taken their toll. Compared with Cotton Davidson, he looked like he was working in slow motion. It was difficult for him even to throw short sideline patterns. He didn't look well, either. Never much of a physical specimen, Lenny looked sapped, pale, and pained.

An old friend of mine, Lank Smith, was a prominent attorney in Dallas. He was also an old Notre Dame player, and he came out to watch us practice that first week in camp. After observing Lenny for a while, he took me aside.

"My God, Hank. I saw Dawson play against us at Notre Dame. I can't believe he has deteriorated so much. This is dreadful. I know you're not going to like hearing this, but I'm telling you, you had better dump this guy, 'cause I guarantee that if you get emotionally involved and sentimental about keeping him, well, you're going to lose your job, sure as hell."

He wasn't alone in his tough judgment; others whispered the same advice. I kept telling myself that Leonard was sterling, just tarnished. All he needed was some polish. I also prayed a lot. Losing my job—any job—was a lousy prospect, but Lenny's not recovering his skills would be downright tragic.

What the heck, I thought. Bobby Layne had been hopelessly dead-ended as a rookie quarterback on the Bears and traded, then moved with the hapless Boston Yanks to New York (where they were renamed the Bulldogs) before he finally joined the Lions and found his fame. Baltimore, once upon a time, had cut John Unitas. Hard knocks went with the game. I filmed Lenny in practice, then reviewed the footage with him. We went back to basics, and I coached him on mechanics.

Training camp was drawing to an end. Before the final cuts, Bunker Hunt, Lamar, and I privately exchanged our personal lists of those we thought would make the team that year. (There was no purpose to this other than curiosity.) Neither Lamar nor Bunker had Leonard Dawson's name on his list.

In preseason play I used Lenny very sparingly, and I watched him closely in practice. It was obvious, to me at least, that his footwork and timing were coming back. He was getting into the pocket and setting up faster and faster. He didn't do anything spectacular in the exhibition games, but I could feel him getting stronger and better. In the final preseason game he did a good job, and I decided to take the chance of starting him in the opener of the '62 season.

It was against the Patriots in the Cotton Bowl. I said a special prayer for my quarterback that day and held my breath as the kickoff arched overhead. The decision to start Lenny had been less than unanimously supported. The Texans took the field for their first offensive series. I stood on the sideline and waited. Leonard went back to pass, and I could sense it—that cold fire was there in him again. He was in control; he was in his element.

Lenny threw three touchdown passes and decimated Boston, 42–28. Lenny Dawson was back.

His teammates gave Leonard a nickname inspired by his penchant for staying clean in the rather soiling occupation of pro football. They called him Ajax. "Like the Greek warrior?" a sportswriter asked one of the linemen. "Naw, as in scouring powder," the teammate explained.

Leonard was clearly going to be the starting quarterback, but I still wanted Cotton Davidson and Eddie Wilson behind him. Lamar Hunt, however, traded Cotton for a draft choice in 1963, and did so without consulting me, breaking our agreement that I would have complete control of such decisions. I was furious. It would leave us with only a rookie backing up Lenny. But after I cooled off, I realized why he had done it. I was too close to Cotton, very attached to him. Also, the player Lamar had traded for was one of the best young tackles anywhere, Junious "Buck" Buchanan. I had to admit it was a real coup, made possible only by the new talent scout on our staff, Don Klosterman. Don said Buchanan could run a 220 in twenty seconds flat with a goat under each arm, and he was right. Buck was big and amazingly fast.

The team was really taking shape with the addition of Fred Arbanas, Johnny Robinson, Jerry Mays, Tyrer, and now Buck Buchanan. We also gathered up Curtis McClinton from the University of Kansas, Frank Jackson, and, of course, E. J. Holub.

The Dallas Texans were changing, growing. The only thing that didn't change was the attitude toward our modest modifications in strategies and formations. My good friend Sid Gillman, head coach of the rival Chargers, took me to task about our I-formation.

"It will never go in professional football," he insisted. "It's a college formation: it's not a good passing formation. It'll never be successful in pro ball."

I thanked him for his advice and kept on using it. Meanwhile, Don Klosterman had some advice of his own for me. We had hired him away from the San Diego Chargers to chase down talent for us. (Lance Alworth, Keith Lincoln, Ernie Ladd, and John Hadl were some of his finds.) One afternoon he came by to watch our workout and said, "Hey, don't you use a concealed area to practice?"

Don was astonished that we didn't and insisted Sid Gillman, for one, was watching every one of our practices before his Chargers played us. As a result, we put a big fence around our practice field. We also deployed someone to skunk Sid Gillman's workouts, a marine officer named Colonel Frank Barnes, who was stationed nearby in San Diego. He would just go out there in his uniform, and no one ever said a word. Then, during our games, Sid and I would pace opposite sidelines like two gentlemen sportists beneath reproach.

Sid Gillman and I were great friends. Before every game we would spot one another on the field somewhere and march toward each other like gunfighters. When we finally came together, we bumped bellies instead of shaking hands.

He would say, "Let me see that game plan, Dapper."

I had it rolled up in my hand usually and would hand it right over. Sid would examine it, throw it on the ground, and pretend to step on it.

"It'll never work," he'd said, laughing, and off he'd go back to his side of the field to try to beat our brains out. Which is exactly where we found ourselves in the fourth game of the season, facing Sid's Chargers.

We had won three straight until we ran into Sid Gillman's team and were beaten 32–28 in a classic shootout. The Texans came right back, winning the next seven games and losing only two, but not before Chris Burford caught a slant pass and took a hit that tore up his knee. I decided to adjust our style to the new situation by abandoning our multiple formations. We went with two tight ends instead, and two flankers. We finished the regular schedule against the Chargers and *beat* them, 26–14.

We were 11 and 3 and scheduled for the final game—the AFL championship—but without Burford, our finest wide receiver and one of the best in all football even at that early stage of his career. We did have Tommy Brooker, though, a fine tight end from Alabama.

The opposition was the 1960 American League champs, the Houston Oilers.

Tommy Brooker and Fred Arbanas were at tight end. Our big fullback, Curtis McClinton, was the lone back, alternating with Jack Spikes, and Abner Haynes and Frank Jackson played flanker. The plan was simple. Houston's coach, Pop Ivy, favored a double-wing formation, lots of sets, and lots of motion. He also liked his backs to blitz often. I thought two tight ends could neutralize their blitz, leaving the remaining defensive backs to go man-for-man against our flankers, both of whom had great outside speed.

Tommy Brooker, who was also our kicker, made a 25-yard field goal to put us three up on the Oilers, followed by a 28-yard touchdown pass from Dawson to Abner Haynes, and a 2-yard plunge by Abner for a second score. At the half we led 17–0.

George Blanda came out in the third quarter behind a slot double-wing. We were playing it safe, trying to protect our big lead with zone coverage, and old George just picked at the soft spots, patiently taking the short yardage we were conceding. They moved steadily down to our 15, where he hit his tight end, Willard Dewveall, for a touchdown. It was the only score of the quarter.

The fourth quarter seemed a repeat, with nobody scoring. With eleven minutes to go and the Texans leading 17–7, old George kicked a 31-yard field goal. It was 17–10.

We got a little rain and the field grew progressively worse. Like some thoroughbreds, however, George Blanda was a great mudder and was just enjoying himself no end as he marched his guys deep into our territory and put Charley Tolar across the goal line from the 1. George's point-after kick tied the game, 17–17. Nothing happened in the next five minutes, and we went into a fifth-quarter overtime. A kick would probably decide the championship.

. Our offense had produced zero points for two quarters, and our punting wasn't the world's best, so I decided that, if we won the toss, we would elect to kick, and defend with the wind at our backs. Well, the officials were nervous—and the players too. We won the toss, but referee Red Born made a simple mistake in not enumerating the proper options for Abner Haynes, and we wound up kicking from the wrong end and *into* the wind.

The Oilers were elated, Abner was stunned. It could have happened to anybody. The tension level in the stands and on the field was tremendous, the players were exhausted and fired-up at the same time.

"Abner," I said, "listen. Forget about it. *Everybody,* forget about it. It's ancient history. We still got to win the game. That's the only thing that's important. Win the game!"

Well, nobody scored in the first overtime, and we went into a second overtime. Lenny took over. He hit Jack Spikes with a short pass and put the ball on the Oilers' 38, then sent Jack over left tackle to their 19 on a counterplay. We ran three more plays, really just to put the ball in position for a kick from the 25.

The field was sloppy, and I was worried about how well Tom Brooker might do, kicking on that muddy surface.

"Tommy," I said on the sideline, "make sure you keep your head down and still, and kick it through."

"Don't worry, Coach," he shot back, "I'll kick that sucker right through there." And he did!

The Dallas Texans were the AFL champs, winning the longest game ever played in professional football. Lenny Dawson, the leading passer in the league, was voted its Most Valuable Player, and Curtis McClinton, our great fullback, was voted Rookie of the Year.

SEVEN

LAMAR and his wife separated and later divorced. After a while, Lamar began dating. One night we double-dated. Lamar's date was the cowgirl who had won the Renault for selling more tickets than anybody else, a wonderful gal named Norma Knoble. We had a great time together that night, and both Phyllis and I felt sure she was going to be the No. 1 draft choice. And so it turned out.

Norma was a schoolteacher—bright, intelligent, enthusiastic. She had a sensational personality, and we loved her. Lamar did too. He proposed, and she accepted. Then he asked me for a favor: Would I be the best man?

At the appointed time, about an hour before the ceremony, Phyllis and I picked up Lamar. It was ten o'clock in the morning on the campus of SMU, where he was reliving an under-graduate-like, bachelor existence. He came piling out of his apartment with a couple of suitcases and lots of loose clothes.

"Where," I said, "are you taking this stuff?" I pointed at the clothes and things draped across his shoulders and pinned under his arms.

"On my honeymoon," he said. They were honeymooning in Austria and taking in the Olympics.

"Gee," I said, "are you going to carry it like this on the plane?"

"Well, we'll get it organized as we go. If we need to, we'll buy some luggage along the way," he said, and proceeded to throw all his stuff into the trunk. It looked like a garage sale back there. Phyllis looked at me; she couldn't believe it.

At half past ten we were finally loaded up and on our way to the small ceremony awaiting us in Richardson, Texas, a nearby town. Fifteen minutes down the highway, we turned off toward the community where Norma lived.

Lamar said, "Ah, pull over here for a minute."

"Lamar! We haven't much time."

"We've got time, we've got time. Just pull over there."

In front of an ice cream parlor is where he had me stop.

"Do you want a cone?" he asked.

"Yeah," I said, "one pistachio and one chocolate chip."

We made it on time anyway, and I stood up for Lamar. After the wedding, Norma waited patiently by the neat pile of her properly packed and tagged luggage while Lamar transferred his stuff from my car to the trunk of theirs, tossing it all in. He grinned, shook my hand, and they were off.

Weeks later they returned and took up residence in a beautiful colonial home in University Park, right off the SMU campus he so loved. The house was great, but they had little furniture except in the bedroom; they were having fun decorating the place a room at a time. They invited me to stay over one night, and Lamar took me up to my bedroom. In the closet on the third floor, I found a five-gallon water bottle half-filled with a lot of coins. It was his way of trying to save some money—by putting it down the narrow neck into the huge bottle. Why keep it on the third floor?

"Well," Lamar said, "I don't get as much exercise as I should, so this makes me walk up the three flights and back down. I figure I derive two benefits at the same time."

I nodded. "Right." And I went downstairs to the den. I turned on the television, and the picture was black and white. I fiddled with the dial, but nothing helped. Norma came in.

"Norma, is this set broken?"

"No, why?"

71

"It's black and white on all the channels."

"I know," she said. "It's a black-and-white set." She sighed. "Lamar promised me a new color TV if you win the championship this year, so I really hope you win that title."

"Yeah," I said. "Me too."

Lamar loved SMU, and he loved Dallas, as did most every player on the Texans. So it came as quite a shock when he told me the team was moving. He was finally convinced that Dallas could not support two clubs.

"Okay," I said, "but why us? Why not them? We've won the title. Let *them* leave town. They've barely won *any* games. *They* are the losers. Who wants to see a losing team?"

"Yes," he said, "but who would *buy* a losing team and move it?"

He had me there. We were attractive precisely because we had won a championship and lit up the city for a season. Ironically, it was that very excitement, much of it nationally televised, that tempted them to pursue the franchise. New Orleans had been the prime candidate, but Tulane University, worried about the competition with its collegiate program, denied permission to use the Sugar Bowl. Meanwhile, the mayor of Kansas City had guaranteed Lamar a minimum sale of twenty-five thousand season tickets. The deal was sealed. The Dallas Texans were moving to K.C.

Lamar was heartsick, he hated so to see us leave. So was I. I loved Dallas; I loved what we had accomplished here, as did the players. They had bought homes here, settled their families; a good number were from the area, and several had been born and raised in Big D. Jerry Mays threatened to retire. Hell, who could blame him. We had sold a lot of the players on the Texans by using Dallas as a main attraction. Now we weren't even going to be able to keep the resurrected team name we had worked so hard to establish: The "Kansas City Texans" just wasn't going to wash.

Once again I left Phyllis and our six kids behind, at our home on North Haven Road, and set out for Kansas City with my car loaded with clothes and belongings. I was the last person in the organization to leave and literally had to pull over at one point, because I couldn't see to drive through the tears. On paper we looked likely to repeat as champs of the AFL, but I wondered. We were going to lose people over this, I was sure, and the mood of those remaining was not going to be good.

On May 14 the move was announced, and the Dallas Texans became the Kansas City Chiefs. The rest didn't go nearly as smoothly. The promised twenty-five thousand season seats turned out to be thirteen thousand, housing for the black players was a problem, and a lot of the guys were disgruntled, to put it politely. Still, everyone tried to do his level best. A new addition, Stone Johnson, helped a lot in many respects. He was special, a world-class Olympic track star, our Mr. Lightning— a speed receiver. He was also brand-new and enthusiastic, something all of us appreciated under the circumstances. My eldest son, Hank, was especially fond of him, and when the youngster came to camp in Missouri, he and Stone would walk to the nearby town of Liberty and get an ice cream. They talked a lot and were close friends.

Stone Johnson went in to return a kickoff in a preseason game we were playing in Wichita against the Oilers. But the ball went to another young back, Preacher Pilot, from the University of New Mexico. Being the team player he was, Stone Johnson tried to block for Preacher. He threw a block but didn't make very good contact. He hit the tackler with his head and the back of his neck. We rushed him to the hospital. He had broken his neck, the doctors told us. Dale, my other son, and Hank went with me to see him in the hospital, and it was clear he was badly hurt, paralyzed from the waist down. I felt sick inside.

Stone remained in Wichita, too seriously hurt to be moved, and we kept in daily touch with the hospital. Then one morning, his doctor called and said Stone Johnson had passed away.

I was a pallbearer at the funeral in Dallas. Hank junior, nine years old, had cried like I had never seen him cry and asked me to bring him a memento from the service.

"Dad," he said, weeping as I held him, "how could this happen? I thought football was just a game."

I brought him back a rose and the program from Stone's funeral. Hank pressed the flower in his prayer book, where it remains to this day.

We tried to restore ourselves, but it just wouldn't happen. The combination of the move and the tragedy of Stone Johnson's death had drained everyone, especially Abner Haynes. I had always thought him to be a carefree, flamboyant, fun-loving guy. Now I saw how sensitive and caring he was—and also very religious. He was, after all, a preacher's son and very close to his family, and to his brother, Sam, in Dallas. Sam had been at every practice and every game, something no longer possible. Abner had also been very close to Stone, and he just couldn't get over what had happened. Suddenly, the previous season's leading rusher of the AFL, and its record-breaking scorer, lost it. Something had gone out of him; he just wasn't the same. Maybe none of us were.

We managed to win our first game in a big way, tied the second game, and lost the next, and the next, and the next. . . . Lenny's jersey was often caked with dirt now. It was a young team—the average age was twenty-three—and it seemed to have left its heart in Dallas.

Nor did the citizens of K.C. take us to their bosom so readily. The stands were sparsely populated. It was hard to sell our guys on the idea that we belonged in Kansas City. Only toward the year's end did we rally and start to win some games.

Just a few days before our next-to-last game, Fred Arbanas was jumped by some rowdies downtown and hit in the eye. We left for the coast without him. A half hour before the kickoff, the grounds keeper summoned me to the telephone in his shed. It was Fred's doctor back in Kansas City; Fred needed an immediate operation. There was damage at the back of the eyeball and he would lose most of his vision in that eye. It was heartbreaking news. I suddenly felt as a lot of the players did—jinxed.

Arbanas was a great tight end, a young guy at the beginning of his career. Now this. Back home, I kept mulling it over. I went to see Fred in the hospital to try and console him; he was downcast. What could I do? I felt so helpless. I took my sons Dale and Stu outside in our front yard and had them throw me passes while I ran Fred's tight-end patterns wearing a patch on one eye. To my great joy, I found that I could see the ball well enough to catch it if I turned my head a little to the inside; and when I lined up on the side of my "good" eye, I could locate the ball immediately. Elated, I ran into the house and called Fred in the hospital with the news. We would work on it, he would play again, I told him, and his spirits seemed to lift.

We packed up the team for New York and the last game. The New York Titans had folded, reemerging as the Jets under Weeb Ewbank. We beat them and finished the year with five wins, seven losses, and two ties. A losing season. We also lost our superstar back in a trade to the Broncos.

Scorer of twenty-two touchdowns the year before, leading rusher and scorer in the league, Abner Haynes was gone, traded. I thought it would be better for him, I knew it would be better for us. And I did it.

I almost left, myself. Andy Gustafson, my old head coach at Miami, called and invited me to Florida. It was about a job, of course. I went down, and he offered me the head coaching spot at the University of Miami; Andy was kicking himself upstairs.

The offer was tempting, but I thought I owed it to Lamar to discuss it with him. We had a long talk about my misgivings. He changed my mind. I decided to stay, but I wasn't sure I was glad about it.

Don Klosterman helped tremendously. Once a star quarterback at Loyola in Los Angeles, he was a remarkable talent hunter and had a droll sense of humor. People liked and trusted him right off and had great respect for his knowledge. Besides, as head coach I couldn't really socialize with the players; I could run around with Don, though. I loved playing practical jokes on him, and he could talk football all day and night and knew everybody in the game.

It's amazing what a brilliant coach you can be and how often you will win if your guys are bigger, faster, and stronger than the opposition's. Don was a genius at signing the biggest and the best, which, in the AFL-versus-NFL player wars of the mid-sixties, was no mean feat. The competition was fierce, no holds barred.

Whether a high draft pick or an unknown and unheralded player from some obscure college, Don would find him and sign him. Buck Buchanan, for example, had been everyone's high selection, but Don got him to sign with us. Heisman winner Mike Garrett was another star he bagged. Although the youngster was a risk because of his small size, Don Klosterman—typically—gambled on his great talent. In his usual daring way, Don signed up Garrett right under the nose of the NFL, at half time in an East-West game—on national television, no less. Don was aided and abetted by scout Lloyd Wells, a onetime Houston sportswriter.

We signed Frank Pitts from Southern University and Gloster Richardson from Jackson State, and we were going after Gale Sayers and Otis Taylor. Sayers, in fact, was married to a girl from K.C. and he told us he was definitely signing with the Chiefs, when suddenly Buddy Young of the NFL flew into town and simply made off with him. Meanwhile, we got word that Otis Taylor was being staked out too, and we put Lloyd Wells on the case, quick.

Lloyd hurried back from scouting a Tennessee State game and combed Dallas for Otis, whom he knew well. From Otis Taylor's mother in Houston, he got Otis's girlfriend's telephone number in Dallas and called. Lloyd pleaded with her, and she finally revealed that Otis was in a motel in Richardson, Texas. Lloyd drove right over, only to find a gaggle of security men from the NFL milling around, and a good many pro scouts socializing with a lot of college players. Lloyd slipped a camera around his neck and passed himself off as a photographer for *Jet* magazine on a story assignment. The security men bought it, and Lloyd got to Taylor's room, where he confronted the young man. Otis agreed to leave with Lloyd but couldn't walk away from the NFL's social directors. They would rendezvous later and make their getaway.

At two o'clock that morning, Lloyd returned to the motel. Several burly fellows intercepted him and ordered him to leave. If he didn't, he had the choice of going to jail or being shot. Lloyd sped away. The two guys, however, followed. Spotting a nightclub, Lloyd pulled up in front. He sweet-talked a young waitress, who was just leaving, into pretending they had a date. He would drive her home. The trick worked, and he headed back to the motel.

Parking in back, he jumped a fence, sneaked past the motel pool, and knocked on the sliding-glass patio door of Otis's room. With Otis was his best friend, Seth Cartwright, a big tackle. What the heck, thought Lloyd, and he smuggled them both out the back and over the fence. By the time they reached the Dallas airport, it was dawn. When Lloyd spotted a couple of suspicious-looking guys making inquiries at the check-in counter, he did a quick about-face back into his car and drove them all to the airfield in Forth Worth, flew them directly to Kansas City, and delivered them personally to Don Klosterman.

Otis Taylor wanted a Thunderbird as an enticement to sign, and he got it. Seth Cartwright, his pal, wanted a barrel of money, and we packed him off to the Jets, who signed him the next day.

In addition to such prominent players, Lloyd also turned up unsung and undrafted youngsters like Mack Lee Hill, a back from Texas Southern. Lloyd insisted he was a genuine sleeper. Still, he had signed him for a mere three-hundred-dollar bonus. If he was so good, I wondered, why hadn't anyone else in either league pursued him? Lloyd just kept saying, "This kid can run the football." I watched Mack Lee Hill closely in practice. The kid could run the football; Lloyd was absolutely right. Mack Lee was the Cinderella Kid, a potentially great player right out of nowhere.

Pete Beathard of USC, Ed Lothamer of Michigan, Bobby Bell, Aaron Brown—Don Klosterman and Lloyd Wells brought us some fine ones. Unfortunately for the Chiefs, Don had little fondness for the general manager, a very ambitious financial man named Jack Steadman, by whom he eventually got himself fired over a crack he made about Kansas City. K.C., Don said, wasn't heaven or hell, but more like purgatory. It was witty and funny, and the remark made the papers. Don was out.

In the meantime, ticket sales were still a problem Lamar kept trying to solve. In our second year in K.C. he came up with the idea, for an exhibition game, of having me call the plays from the press box over the radio. Everyone in the stands would be invited to bring their portables and listen in. Meanwhile, the quarterbacks would have microphones and headsets as well. The fans would be able to hear me and them. It was a preseason game for rookies and quarterbacks and would be a lot of fun, he said.

I resisted. "I really don't think it's a good idea."

"Why not?" Lamar said, looking puzzled.

"You never know what's going to be said on the sidelines or in the huddle. I don't like it."

Lenny Dawson, he argued, didn't use profanity, and neither did Head Coach Stram. Reluctantly, I agreed to the experiment. Lamar was very pleased and began advertising the game and his gimmick. It seemed to work. A nice crowd turned out, and nearly everyone was carrying a portable radio.

The scrimmage was against the Broncos, and it went well. We were closing in for a touchdown toward the end of a drive, when I decided to put in rookie quarterback Sandy Stephens. Over the radio, I called a sweep to the right side. Stephens repeated the call in the huddle.

"Fifty-two pop. G O. On three." Then added, "Okay, you sons 'a bitches, let's get this mother in the end zone."

You could hear oohs and ahs all through the stadium.

One morning that spring I was awakened at three by the phone. It was the emergency room at the hospital. One of my players, Ed Budde, was there, severely injured. I sped over and dashed into the emergency area. The attendants were having difficulty restraining Budde, who was a mess, bleeding profusely from his ears, nose, and mouth. He had gotten into a fight at a local bar, and a second guy had struck him repeatedly on the head with a lead bolt. Whether he would be able to play football appeared academic. Whether he'd survive and lead a normal life seemed more pertinent. God, it seemed like open season on football players.

Harassment in public from unhappy or rival fans went with the job. So did challenges from barstool jocks. In K.C.'s more colorful neighborhood emporiums, these types were no joke. K.C. was not far removed from its frontier heritage; as towns went, it was tough. But so was its football team.

Finally they subdued Budde and rushed him into surgery. He pulled through, but his career was history, I thought. Poor Ed. The operation had left him with a metal plate in his skull.

Budde had other ideas. With a gumption that was fast becoming the Chiefs' trademark, Ed recovered his health, suited up, and went back to the AFL's trenches.

Guts were what the Chiefs were about—guys like Ed and E. J. Holub. E.J. was from football country: Lubbock, Texas, where he had been an outstanding high school center and linebacker. And a Catholic! He looked like a solid prospect for Notre Dame back in the mid-fifties, and I was just about to go and recruit him for Terry Brennan's Fighting Irish when the order was rescinded because Holub already had a pair of bad knees. Nobody thought they could hold up, even in college competition. Notre Dame passed him up. E.J. went to Texas Tech instead and became a two-time All-American and the most sought-after player in the '61 draft. We picked him No. 1 and got him. From the first day you could see he was just a great athlete and the quintessential football player.

He was the perennial rookie, always up, always there. By his own account he wasn't a leader—though he was, of course. Instead, he saw himself as a pusher, constantly hollering, encouraging, staying on people in that likable way of his. He loved the game and played it with the abandon of a kid and the knees of an old man. Every year he would injure them and keep on playing; and every off-season he would have them operated on, for a total of eleven knee operations (not counting the six in college).

He would always have his surgery done in Lubbock, because he had a lot of confidence in Dr. Henry there. I'd call after the operation to see how he felt and how long they were intending to keep him. The usual prediction was a week, but invariably he would be gone the following morning, escaped back to his ranch and his horses. He and his wife and two beautiful daughters lived so far in the woods, they didn't even have a phone, which is the way he preferred it. To reach him, you had to call a neighbor and give him a message; and then E.J. would call back. That's how you kept in touch with him in the off-season. But each year, back he would come to training camp, on time and ready to go. He never missed a game or a practice. He always found a reason to be there, no matter how much he was hurting.

Typically, I would ask trainer Wayne Rudy about him and be put off.

"Well, now," Wayne would say, "I don't truly think Holub should practice, but you know how E.J. is. I don't know. I'll have to tell you later," he'd say, looking suspicious.

Once I caught Wayne abetting Holub. The door to the trainer's room was closed, and when I pushed it open, to ask him about E.J., the trainer gave me an odd look and glanced back into the room. There was Holub, sitting doubled up on the table, with his knees under his chin, trying to hide behind the door.

"Listen, E.J.," I said, "if your knees are bothering you, don't come out to practice. It's better to miss a day now than to miss the game on Sunday."

"Well, thanks, Coach. I appreciate that, but I think I'll be fine."

"Are you sure you can practice?"

"Yes, sir. Oh, yeah, yeah. Oh, I'll be fine. I'll be out there. Don't you worry none."

Wayne Rudy would drain 110 cubic centimeters of fluid from E.J.'s swollen knees, and out he'd come. He was a sensational outside linebacker, and later, when his knees became too bad, he anchored the team at center. He just never quit.

He was a cowboy at heart: He loved horses, loved his ranch, the wide-open spaces. At the end of the season, he'd stop by the house in his pickup truck. It would be early morning. He'd make a lot of noise and wake us all. Phyllis would fill him up with pancakes and eggs, then he'd jump back in his truck.

"Coach," he'd say, "I'll be in touch." But he wouldn't.

After every season he disappeared. We never heard anything more of him, but when the weather turned warm and July approached, you just knew E. J. Holub was somewhere out there in that Texas brush, saddling up.

EIGHT

FRED Arbanas spent a lot of the off-season catching passes. He and Len Dawson worked together, starting out slowly, then increasing the distance and the intensity of their workouts. By the opening of the '65 season I knew Fred was ready.

Ed Budde was whole again, E. J. Holub had another "good-as-new" knee and a new scar, and Jerry "Captain Huzza" Mays was exhorting everyone to perform. The Kansas City fans started to come around. Their change in attitude was mostly due to a free agent, 235-pound Mack Lee Hill, the unknown kid Lloyd Wells had signed out of Southern University. He won the job as starting fullback and was looked upon locally as the first true Kansas City Chief and not some Dallas exile.

Mack Lee was a coach's dream. He just seemed able to run into pileups and out the other side. His hard running drew the crowds. They cheered him like a hometown hero, even the self-styled "wolf pack" that howled and booed us so mercilessly.

It was the same with Pete Beathard, our popular rookie quarterback. He too had done well the previous year, and when Lenny faltered in our opening loss to Oakland, the fans and sportswriters began clamoring for Beathard. Don Klosterman too. In our seventh game I finally made the change given my concern over Lenny's performance. I started Pete Beathard.

Well, he was fired-up, and the Chiefs jumped into a big lead, but then he cooled off, and the Oilers took command. With Houston ahead in the last quarter, I replaced him with Lenny, and Dawson almost pulled the game out with a couple of touchdown passes. A field goal beat us, 38–36.

After that game it was clear to me that I had to decide on who our No. 1 quarterback would be and stay with him as the starter. It was incredibly difficult. Pete was young, sometimes terrific, but not progressing quickly enough to take over. Lenny knew the team system and had the respect of the players. He was the oldest player on the team and had a steadying influence. I decided to stick with Leonard and take the heat.

With Lenny at the helm, we were on our way to a 7-5-2 record when disaster struck again. In the next-to-last game at Buffalo, Mack Lee Hill caught a screen pass and took a hard hit from the Bills' linebacker. He was taken off the field with an injured knee and examined on the bench. The team doctor was sure he would need an operation, but after the game Mack Lee dismissed all thoughts of surgery. Like a lot of athletes, he didn't like medications or hypodermics and just wanted to let his knee heal by itself.

We tried to convince him that the ligaments and cartilage weren't about to mend without intervention, and he finally seemed persuaded. Holub had chalked up a dozen such procedures; other players had had them too. In football they went with the territory. The knee just wasn't made to take the punishment of the game, and this was one of the prices you paid if you were going to keep on playing. The doctors said it would be just like new. Mack seemed convinced.

The Monday after the game, I was in my office, both doors wide open. Mack Lee hobbled by, paused, and limped away when he saw me on the phone. He came back a second time. I was still on the phone but quickly hung up and called out to him.

"Mack, we've arranged for you to be admitted to the hospital tonight at six, and you'll be operated on at ten o'clock tomorrow morning. I talked to the doctors, and everything is all set. They don't expect any problems whatsoever.''

"Coach, the more I think about it, the more I really think I could get by without an operation—''

"Mack! Mack. We talked about this. You're only fooling yourself. It's just wishful thinking. You've gotta have the operation. That's all there is to it.''

He agreed, but six o'clock came and Mack Lee hadn't shown up at the hospital. I checked again. By eight I was concerned and tried to call him. There was no answer. Nine o'clock, the same story. At ten a young woman called, Mack Lee's girlfriend. She was a nurse and had been talking to him for hours, trying to coax him to the hospital. She was calling to say they were on their way there; Mack had finally agreed to be admitted. I was relieved and thanked her for her help.

The next morning I was in coaches' meetings, getting ready to face our last opponent of the season. Everyone was anxious to hear how our young starting fullback was doing. So was I. A call from Joe Lichtor, the team doctor, took me from the meeting. As soon as I heard him, I knew there was trouble.

"Coach, I have terrible news.'' Joe was having a hard time controlling his voice. "Mack Lee Hill died on the operating table. Hypothermia. His temperature soared to one hundred seven.''

Before he got through explaining how this freakish thing had happened, I was in tears. I was so shocked. I didn't know what to say or what to think. I just sat there, staring, totally stunned.

I wanted to cancel the last game and called Lamar. He felt the same way and concurred. Everyone was grief-stricken. The next day, however, we decided to play the upcoming final game after all. We decided to play it in his memory. The following year his teammates instituted an award in his name, an award for the rookie who most exemplified his spirit.

The team was still young, with an average age of twenty-five years and four months. Lenny was the only one over thirty. But Mack Lee's passing aged everyone. It was a tough and sober team that came to camp the next summer. I had invited

Father Mackey to join us once again for a few weeks, and he sensed it too. His usual demonstration of marathon-walking styles drew laughs, and the guys responded warmly to his leading them in calisthenics and such, but there was something different about the 1966 Chiefs. They were steely—determined. So was I.

We had the talent, and we had the tactics. We had defensive alignments that were difficult for offenses to handle, including the triple-stack, something I had cooked up and first tried out in '62. Instead of four linebackers lining up in the slots between the linemen, they lined up behind them: the right linebacker behind the right tackle, another behind the nose tackle, one behind the other tackle, and another behind the defensive end. It made the linebackers very hard to get to and presented the offensive line with some serious blocking dilemmas. Once again, other coaches were critical. I didn't care. We won, and that's all that counted. It worked.

I had also added the moving pocket as a permanent fixture in our offense. Like almost everything in football, it was born out of adversity—adversity in the form of Ernie "the Cat" Ladd, 325 pounds and six feet nine and his similarly massive sidekick, Earl Faison, late of the San Diego Chargers. They were awesome and contributed more than their share to beating us three times in a row at one point.

The moving pocket, I hoped, might foil them and check their patented rush. It consisted simply of Lenny Dawson rolling to one side or the other and only occasionally dropping straight back in the conventional way passers moved into the hedge of protective linemen. We would also fake a back into the line on most passing plays: play action.

I put in the moving pocket in '64 against the Chargers. Fred Arbanas would block down on Earl Faison from his end position, while the tackle went at him low, where he didn't like being hit. Then the tackle would block down on Ernie Ladd with our guard. We would roll to that side, and Lenny would set up seven yards behind the tight end and throw. So there wasn't the usual big straight-ahead pass-rush at a basically stationary target. In fact, with Ladd and Faison tangled up, it left only the linebacker on that side to contend with, and we still had our fullback to block him if he blitzed. If he didn't, the fullback would slide out into the flat. The first time we sprang it on San Diego, it worked beautifully. It just destroyed their out-containment. Lenny completed his first eleven passes, and Frank Jackson caught four for touchdowns. They never knew what hit 'em, and we trampled them 49–6.

By 1966 we had more offensive alignments than any team in professional football—sixty-five different formations, all emanating from the tight-I. We used from one to two dozen per game. On defense, instead of the usual 4-3, we had six different alignments, zone coverage, and man-for-man. These were executed by a team I wouldn't want to face, no matter what their formation: Buck Buchanan over the center (six feet seven, 287 pounds), Sherrill Headrick, E. J. Holub, Bobby Bell, Smokey Stover, Walt Corey, Jerry Mays. It was one fierce crew.

The Chiefs had a unique look and a lot of versatility. But people win games, not formations and alignments. Sooner or later, in every game, it got down to where you had to take it to the other team physically. Contact. It didn't matter how cunning a game plan you had, or how many formations, if the other guy could beat you physically. I looked over the class of '66 and sensed they were ready for just about anybody.

We won all our exhibition games and opened against the Bills in Buffalo. They had beaten us the last four meetings. We started off passing from a new double-wing formation, then worked our backs against them: Curtis McClinton at full, Bert Coan and Mike Garrett at half, and Lenny Dawson. Final score: 42–20! A great start.

The next week, we beat Oakland 32–10 in their aromatic stadium and headed for Boston. Monsignor Mackey joined us on the bench, as usual, and we downed the Patriots, 43–24. Smug, we flew back to Kansas City and took on the Bills again. We were overconfident and we lost, but this team was not about to fold. We were 4-2 and on the road again. We took on the Broncos on their home field and really put it to them. By the fourth quarter we were winning 42–10, and the Denver fans were expressing their indignation with a shower of beer cans and bottles and whatever else was handy.

I took out Lenny Dawson and put in Pete Beathard with instructions to run the ball as much as he could, to use up the remaining time so we could just finish and get the hell out of town. Well, the two rookie backs I had put in were so excited at their chance on the field that they bumped into each other on the first play, totally confusing the defense. Pete Beathard, meanwhile, unable to hand off, had been left holding the ball, so to speak. For want of anything better to do, he rolled out to the right and just kept going, all the way to a touchdown.

The place went crazy. Ray Malavasi, the Denver coach, was enraged. All kinds of things came flying through the air. On the sideline I gathered the kicking team and told them, listen, let's kick an onside kick, because we don't want the ball in their end zone near the especially fanatical Bronco fans. I instructed them to be sure to *tell* the Broncos, so they could fall on the ball at their 40 and have it till the end of the game. So our kicker, Mike Mercer, set up the football and was hollering, "Onside kick! Onside kick!" The Broncos responded with some choice epithets and uncomplimentary gestures. Mercer kicked it onside, as he'd promised, and it hit a surprised Denver man in the leg and ricocheted back toward us. What with all the flailing around, one of our people somehow recovered the ball, and all you could hear for several seconds was a wail of boos. Stuff rained down.

The next thing I knew, our young backs were clipping off yards, and we were in the end zone again. The gun sounded, and we had won, 56–10. I had everyone put on as much equipment as they could, capes and helmets and jackets, and had them walk in a mass out to the middle of the field, turn a hard left, and proceed toward the locker room. As we passed out of the stadium, the fans overhead pelted us with everything imaginable.

I tried to explain to the press what had happened on the busted play and with the onside kick, and everyone just laughed and laughed and didn't believe it for a minute. Denver's coach was livid and called me every name he could think of for running up the score so severely. (Who could make up such a story?)

We made it out of town in one piece and kept on rolling up wins. The Chiefs were having a great year and a great time, and they'd earned both. If ever a team had paid its dues, they had.

When the smoke cleared, the Kansas City Chiefs were in the play-offs for the league championship. We had reached some kind of special level and we were anxious to see just how high it was. This year the sky was the limit, mainly because of Al Davis of the Raiders.

Al Davis is among the most honest people I've ever known. He is also tenacious. When rankled, he is like a force of nature, as the NFL discovered. What had irked Al was the NFL's dismissive attitude toward the AFL and their continued resistance to overtures regarding a merger. Worse, the sports press persisted in painting us as the lesser league because of an alleged disparity in talent. After six years of work, Al and the rest of us felt otherwise. The condescension was unbearable.

Al Davis began agitating for head-on competition, and the heck with any merger. Suddenly, he succeeded Joe Foss as commissioner, and the AFL's role of suitor was abandoned. Instead, Davis challenged the NFL's old guard by recruiting its very best players, people like John Brodie, Mike Ditka, and Roman Gabriel. He was relentless. The NFL owners suddenly saw the light, and a full merger was approved.

Al Davis had been AFL commissioner for sixteen weeks when Lamar Hunt, Pete Rozelle, and Tex Schramm unveiled the peace treaty that instituted a combined draft—to end the bonus wars for talent that were threatening to bankrupt franchises—and set 1970 as the year of full merger. The announcement was made in New York, but Hunt and Schramm had been meeting secretly for months in the parking lot of the Dallas airport, of all places.

Anyway, we were joining the football Establishment, and the internecine warfare was about to begin in earnest. From here on, the best AFL team would meet the best NFL team at the

end of each season to play one game for all the marbles—
the world championship. The Chiefs had come a long way; the
Cowboys too. After five losing seasons, they were also in the
play-offs and would take on Green Bay the same day we faced
Buffalo, the AFL's reigning champs. If we and Dallas both won,
it would be incredible: The two of us in the first Super Bowl.

After losing to Buffalo two years in a row, we had beaten
them once this season but lost to them the second time. Now
we were playing them for the league championship on their home
field. The predictably bad weather favored the Bills. It was just
what they thrived on: wet and freezing. Just to give my guys
some confidence, I matter-of-factly announced in the locker room
that after our win we would stay in town for a party and watch
the NFL fight it out on TV, to see who we would play for the
Super Bowl. Then we would fly back to Kansas City and leave
the following Monday for Los Angeles, site of the world-championship game. The L.A. flight was already booked I informed
them, to loud cheers. With the temperature outside below
freezing, I hoped visions of balmy California in January would
incite them. The ref announced five minutes to the start, and
we took the field.

On the third play of the first quarter, we ran a fake draw play
with a crossing pattern, and Lenny hit Fred Arbanas for a
touchdown. Bang! Jackie Kemp seemed unimpressed with
Leonard Dawson's 29-yard toss. Kemp hit El Dubenion for a
69-yard pass play and a touchdown. We were tied, 7–7.

Lenny moved the Chiefs again and passed to Otis Taylor for
a second touchdown. The defense held the Bills, and taking the
offensive, we pushed them back again but came up short. Still,
Mike Mercer went in and, from 43 yards, banged a field goal
right through the uprights. It was 17–7 at the half; the Chiefs
were on a roll.

After no score in the third, we turned Mike Garrett loose in
the last quarter, and he scored twice on the ground. Final score:
31–7. We had our second league championship. The Chiefs were
11-2-1 on the regular season. At the airport in Kansas City, we
were mobbed by twelve thousand people.

It was Near Year's Day.

I went home and collapsed, but not before unpacking my prize possession and setting it out on the desk in my den. It wasn't much to look at, maybe—eleven inches long and twenty-eight inches around, an inflated rubber bladder encased in leather. But I wouldn't have traded it for the world. The guys had given me the game ball.

I slept like a stone. The next morning I went to the office early and began running the three films we had of our upcoming opponents, winners of the NFL championship for the second straight year; the Green Bay Packers.

Their technique was all too familiar, as was the figure pacing their sideline. Like Vince Lombardi, they were a simple team, yet complicated. Two formations. One defensive alignment. Man-for-man coverage. Simple. Predictable. And the very best. Jimmy Taylor into the weak side, Paul Hornung to the strong side. Paul was a good friend; I had known him at Notre Dame. When had I last seen him? Oh, yeah—a couple of years ago when the Packers had come to Dallas to take on the Cowboys. I went over to one of their workouts that week and found him in the dressing room.

How many people were in the stands? he wanted to know. I told him not many, maybe a thousand.

"Oh, man. I'll get my ass chewed out today," he said, wincing. "Anytime there are a lot of people around, he chews me out something awful. He's got a tough-guy reputation to uphold, you know."

How well I knew. I had watched Lombardi at a practice in 1955 when he was still a Giants assistant coach. I couldn't believe that one man could yell and scream and spout so much profanity. He lashed into everybody except Frank Gifford and Charlie Conerly.

"What was he like in Green Bay?" I asked Paul.

"Never says much up there. But anytime the New York press comes in, or we're on the road and there are a lot of onlookers, he goes through his whole routine. Boy, he yells and screams."

Vince didn't care about strategic planning. He believed you

had to outwork and outmuscle the opposition. If you believed with him, he molded you into the finest football player you could possibly be. If you didn't believe, you were gone. You played his way or else. Lombardi was tough, but he wasn't hard. He was a compassionate man with iron resolve.

I ran the film of the Packers over and over. They did things right and with maximum force. Everyone went all out every second. Still, I was sure we could move the ball on their conservative defense; we outweighed them an average of fifteen pounds per man. Unfortunately, the reverse was true for our defensive unit—their offensive line was bigger.

Switching reels, I put on the Chiefs' win over Buffalo and studied my people. Otis Taylor at flanker: In fourteen games he had racked up over 1,000 yards with forty-eight receptions. Len Dawson led the league in touchdown passes, with twenty-six. Mike Garrett was second in the AFL in rushing, deadly quick to the outside and an escape runner inside, not to mention a great blocker. Bert Coan, the other back—a slasher, six feet four and fast. The great Chris Burford at split end, Fred Arbanas in tight (but probably out now with a shoulder separation). I went over all of them in my mind, considering their qualities, remembering their triumphs and trials. Fred with his one good eye. Lenny with his succession of broken noses. Ed Budde and that plate in his head. E.J. with bad knees and so many banged-out teeth that he'd been nicknamed "Jack-O'-Lantern." Jim Tyrer—the Great Pumpkin—was still at tackle, with Jerry Cornelison. Buck Buchanan, Sherrill Headrick, Bobby Bell, Chuck Hurston, Johnny Robinson, Jerry Mays . . .

Could they do it? I was a coach. I coached them, suffered with them, coaxed, cajoled, prodded, pushed. But I didn't socialize with them, that was the unwritten rule, and I couldn't go out onto the field with them unless someone was hurt, that was the written regulation.

I shut off the projector and picked up the newspaper to try to take my mind off our appointment in L.A., but of course I couldn't resist glancing at the sports page, and the upcoming showdown was splashed all over it. Harry Wismer of the late

91

New York Titans had suggested it be called the Golden Game. Lamar Hunt had another suggestion—Super Bowl. He had been inspired by some Silly Putty his daughter was playing with. She had formed it into a sphere and called it super ball, and it had sparked Lamar.

The powers that be didn't like it and weren't going to use it. In the official literature and programs it was called the World Championship Game, but the press had picked it up and already popularized it, and the Kansas City Chiefs were going to play the Green Bay Packers in the very first Super Bowl. In two weeks it was going to be show-and-tell time.

I put aside the paper and called Father Mackey in Boston. I wanted him there in L.A. with us. We were going to need all the help we could get.

NINE

WE took three days off in Long Beach, and then we began working in secret, practicing the new formations we would throw at the Packers. I coached, cajoled, prodded, pushed. I sincerely believed we could win. We'd have to play the best game of our lives to do so and the challenge was to sell the players on the idea.

The papers, meanwhile, picked Green Bay to win by thirteen points and once again launched into some all-too-familiar comparisons of the AFL with the NFL. The consensus seemed to be that we were the best of the worst, a so-so team from, as one newsman put it, a "Mickey Mouse league."

I gathered my people before practice and said, "Listen. We are now the strong underdog in this game. Let's not say anything to disturb our overrated colleagues who are practicing over in Santa Barbara. Let the sleeping dogs sleep. Let them come in thinking it's going to be easy."

Everybody nodded and obeyed—everybody except "the Hammer." The Hammer was Fred Williamson, a flashy cornerback I'd gotten in a trade from Oakland. He was a seasoned pro but a talker. Fred was an ex-marine, said he knew karate, and proclaimed himself tough at every opportunity. With the media camped out all over the Coast, the opportunities were many, and the Hammer rose to the occasion with typical eloquence. Like Muhammad Ali, he liked to make predictions—such as what he was going to do to Green Bay receivers.

Naturally, the Green Bay coaches plastered their team's quarters and lockers with the Hammer's choice comments, and Fred's teammates were furious. I thought maybe I should send him home and called him in to see what he had to say for himself. A heck of a talker, Williamson laid on an imaginative argument. The team was uptight, he thought, and overly awed by the Packers.

"Hell," he said, "we shouldn't be happy just to be playing in the same game with them. We should be concerned with beating their sorry asses!"

I reprimanded him and ordered him to remain silent from that moment on, not that it probably mattered anymore. *Life* magazine appeared with a story on us, including a close-up feature on Fred and his "Hammer Tackle," which he described as "a blow delivered with great velocity perpendicular to the earth's latitudes." Fred also elaborated on what he would do to receiver Boyd Dowler and some of the other Packers.

Mike Garrett and I were invited to appear on a television variety show. To take my mind off it all, I took Phyllis and the kids to meet Bob Hope, Jimmy Durante, and Bing Crosby before my brief appearance. We all had a great time. I especially envied the ease with which these great performers prepared to go out before millions of onlookers. The head coach of the Chiefs and his team were not nearly as calm about the prospect. We had come to California too early. The two weeks felt like a month.

To keep them up, I invited Frank Leahy to our practices the final week and asked him to say a few words to the guys in his inimitable Boston-Irish brogue, which he graciously did: "Ah, lads, you have a herculean task before you. . . ."

I could see their adrenaline was high; they hadn't slept well in a couple of nights. So on Saturday I sent Bobby Yarborough, our equipment manager, out to buy some props for the next day, when we would set out to beat the Packers. The team was too high, and I had to try and relax them. In point of fact, they had been ready to play days earlier.

When they arrived the next day to suit up, trainers and doctors and equipment people were all wearing Mickey Mouse hats, and a phonograph was playing the Mouseketeers' theme song. Either they'd be infuriated, I figured, or it would loosen them up. Well, it was fun in the locker room, but when we took the field to warm up, I saw that hundreds of Green Bay fans had shared the same inspiration. They were all wearing large-eared hats to taunt the team from the Mickey Mouse league, and I could feel everyone's adrenaline surge and muscles tighten. I looked at Lenny taking his warm-up tosses and he was tight.

Across the field, the Packers looked nonchalant. In fact, while my people had been tossing and turning during the night, a number of the Packer veterans who were certain not to play had gone out on the town and tied one on, Paul Hornung and Max McGee among them. Their teammate, receiver Boyd Dowler, got hurt on the first play of the game, came off the field, and was replaced in the lineup by McGee. Max, a thirty-four-year-old veteran, hadn't expected to see any action at all. He was practically dozing on the bench, enjoying what he thought would be his last time in a Packer uniform before retirement. Terminally hung over, he nearly died when Vince Lombardi sent him in. He didn't know how he could manage to play virtually a whole game. Fate, however, had other plans.

On January 15, 1967, the clock started running on the first Super Bowl. We were the first AFL team ever to face an NFL squad.

There was much more on the line than our pride and bonuses, and we felt the weight of it. We had trouble moving the ball on our first two possessions, and Green Bay scored to lead 7–0. We got the ball and moved it, then stalled, and Mike Mercer trotted in to try a field goal. He missed from 40 yards out, and the quarter ended 7–0. In the second period, Lenny settled down and started picking his way upfield with play-action passes. From 7 yards out, he put a pass into Curtis McClinton's hands in the end zone, and it was all tied up, 7–7. But Green Bay came right back and scored again, regaining the lead.

Lenny led the Chiefs toward their goal line again, but time was running out. Mike Mercer tried a second field goal from the 31 and made it, just as the half ended.

The guys were up; we had done all right. The score was close at 14–10, and the Chiefs were confident. Fred Arbanas, walking toward the locker room, was excited.

"Hey, Coach. Christ, we can beat these guys! They're nothing like we thought they'd be."

The other players felt the same, and I felt good. The versatile, unorthodox Cinderellas were going to beat the staid old hands. We couldn't wait to get back out there.

Lenny opened the second half. Suddenly, the conservative Packers, who never blitzed, blitzed. Lombardi had turned into a fox. Lenny threw the ball, trying to avoid a loss, and it sailed right to Willie Wood, their safety. Willie took off like a rocket for 50 yards, and we didn't catch him until he was on our 5-yard line. Elijah Pitts took care of the remaining yardage, and Green Bay led by 11. One play and it came apart.

Hangover and all, Max McGee then put on a sensational show, making incredible catches all over the place. He pulled in two of Bart Starr's completions for touchdowns and five other passes for good measure. The whole season he had caught a total of three in fourteen games.

The Chiefs didn't score another point. The final tally was a humiliating 35–10. Lombardi's people had won impressively.

We had gone into the game like kids from the wrong side of the tracks, out to prove ourselves and the AFL, and we were going home the way we came. After the game and the hubbub in the locker room, I realized I had misplaced my sons Hank and Dale. I went looking all over for my boys and couldn't find them in the Chiefs' locker area. I asked the equipment manager and the trainer if they had seen them, but they hadn't. What with all the people milling around, I started to worry about their getting lost in the corridors under the Coliseum. Just then I spotted them. They were coming out of the Packers' locker room, loaded down with Green Bay pennants, autographed programs, a game jersey, and even a ball.

"What were you two doing in there?"

Hank junior said: "We went to get autographs of all the famous players. Paul Hornung and Max McGee, Ray Nitschke, Willie Davis. And Bart Starr! Coach Lombardi too. Gee, they were great, Dad." He was flush with excitement.

"And what did Coach Lombardi say to you?"

"Oh, he was very nice. He patted me on the head and said, 'Tell your dad that his team played a good game.'"

Dale, eleven years old, piped up too. "He said he hoped you wouldn't whip us for going in there."

Lombardi tried to be gracious in the postgame interviews as well, and said we had a good team. But he also said that we couldn't compare with the top teams in the NFL, and that there were three or four better than ours.

"There!" he snapped, as he faced the press. "That's what you want me to say, isn't it? There! I've said it."

I felt like we had let the whole American Football League down, not just ourselves. I also resolved that we would be back to settle the score.

The season was over. The staff and players had all gone home to their ranches, insurance businesses, their families. I sat in my office back in Kansas City and toyed with a Polaroid picture taken of one of the defenses employed against us over the course of the year. An assistant had given it to me as a souvenir.

During every game, from the roof of the press box in the end zone, one of our staff took a Polaroid shot of every defensive lineup on every down. Each picture was numbered and the outcome of the play noted. Then the photo was lowered on a wire from the rooftop to the field, and from there a runner rushed it to the bench. In a given game there might be as many as seventy or eighty photos.

I propped the photo against the base of my desk lamp and thought about Vince Lombardi. Green Bay's quarterback had too much time, and ours not enough. We were the deception-and-speed team, yet the Packers had tricked us with the blitz to stop a first-down conversion, and then blitzed us again to ice the game with that interception by Willie Wood.

They—including their coach—were wiser and older, and they had beaten us. Yet Lombardi was wrong. The Chiefs and the other AFL teams could take on the NFL squads anytime. Our styles were different only because the NFL had stood still for so long and resisted new approaches and ideas. With a little more seasoning, we would be ready for a second shot.

I stared at the Polaroid photograph. It had been taken during a game against the Patriots. From down on the field it looked to us as if Boston had gone into an Oklahoma defensive alignment. The Polaroid revealed otherwise. Boston was using our own triple-stack against us.

It seemed to me verification of something about the Chiefs and the AFL and I couldn't help smiling. The Packers and the other NFL teams might be the glorious past, but we were the future. They would have to adjust to *us* at some point, or get left behind.

TEN

PEOPLE thought I was kidding about signing Wilt Chamberlain. Heck, I would have taken him in a second after seeing him handle a football.

It was up at Kutsher's Country Club in Monticello, New York. Wilt and I were both putting in an appearance at a kids' sports clinic near there. Anyway, I had him stand under the crossbar of the goalposts. I told him I was going to throw the football a little above the bar. The first throw touched the bar and bounced on over. Wilt asked me if I wanted him to start catching the ball.

Wilt is seven feet one and nearly three hundred pounds. The crossbar is ten feet off the ground.

"If you don't mind," I said, "yes, please. Catch the ball."

I threw again, and he leaped up, flat-footed, and caught it. I kept throwing. After a bit he was catching the ball with one hand like he was wearing a baseball glove.

How could you possibly defense him? You'd have to have a seven-foot defensive back. Wilt had gone to the University of Kansas too. I was all ready to sign him for the K.C. Chiefs, but his basketball club had other plans for him.

Talent was where you found it, and I was willing to go anywhere for it and consider anyone. In the late sixties, Jim Schaaf, our PR director, and I went to England to audition kickers. We already had the best in pro football, Jan Stenerud, but we thought we might find some good kickers to bring back with us to use as incentives in trading for players. Lamar had a good idea.

The first tryout was in White City Stadium. We set up our portable goalposts and proceeded to test the 110 applicants. Each got three kicks. We lined up the first ten in a row and had them go at it sequentially, while we measured each kick's distance. Number 7 booted the ball about 70 yards. I took a close look at him: Bob Howfield, London. He was a little guy in a brown sweater, slacks, and a beat-up shirt. In the second round of kicks, the seventh man banged it 65 yards, but there was something wrong.

"Hold it, hold it!" I called. "Last time number seven kicked it with his right foot. *You* just kicked it left-footed."

"Yes?" Bob Howfield said, looking surprised. "I kick with both feet, naturally."

"Okay," I said, trying not to look amazed, and we resumed the audition.

We took the tryouts on the road, up to Manchester and to Wales, and returned to White City Stadium with the finalists. Over and over again we had to explain (a) what football was, and (b) that those who qualified could each earn about eight thousand American dollars a year by sitting on a bench during an American football game, trotting in to kick the ball for an extra point or perhaps a field goal from between 20 to 50 yards, then trotting back out to the bench. They couldn't believe that was all they had to do.

We signed the best three and brought them back to the States, including little Bobby Howfield, who wound up with Denver and eventually landed in New York with the Jets, and later came out of retirement to join the Saints.

Cookie Gilchrist was somebody else I went after. Cookie was a dynamic runner with the strength of a bull. He never played college football, yet he managed to star in the Canadian League and then with the Bills. Lou Saban eventually traded him to Denver when Gilchrist became too much to handle. Cookie was a truly gifted back, but he definitely marched to his own drummer. He liked to party and, in the most good-natured way, to flaunt his success. Cookie liked to drive around in his gold Cadillac and call people from it on his gold telephone. He let you know he was what was happening.

I wanted him. Denver's general manager intimated that it might be arranged but that our archrival, Oakland, was aware of our interest. Fearing the introduction of Gilchrist into our lineup, the Raiders had expressed a like interest in acquiring his able services. Negotiations dragged on for weeks as the Raiders and Chiefs vied for Gilchrist, bidding up the price. The Broncos loved it.

We were going nowhere fast when Scotty Sterling, from the Raiders' front office, called with a proposition for a mutually safe solution: "Al Davis told me to tell you that we will lay off if you will lay off."

A Mexican standoff. I agreed. The Raiders broke off their negotiations. Denver called, now suddenly anxious to consummate a deal with us right then and there. No-sense-being-greedy-about-it seemed to be their stance. I declined, much to their dismay. Trading for players was a tricky business.

The Chiefs and Denver Broncos were more successful in dealing for Curley Culp. I had met him at a banquet at Arizona State, where he was the heavyweight wrestling champ. To look at him, he was also just about a perfect guard—except that he didn't want to be. He wanted to play defense.

Denver drafted him as their top pick. They took him as a guard, just as I would have if I hadn't talked to him about it by sheer accident. I sensed we had a shot at him in a trade. However, you don't just call up a rival team about a No. 1 draft choice and inquire if he is available. I bided my time, and sure enough, Denver put him in at guard. He didn't like it, judging from his play, and his coaches weren't impressed. Or so I heard. The right moment had come. I called Bronco coach Lou Saban and asked after a possible backup lineman. We were short a man on offense.

Did I have anyone specifically in mind? No, no, just a spare lineman would do, nobody special. Lou rattled off a list of candidates and included Culp. We haggled, and I agreed to give him a third-round pick in the next draft.

When Culp arrived, I immediately put him on the defense, and he was just great. It was a fine piece of genuine trading, and I was smug about it for days. But as the old saying goes, what goes around comes around. Some years later, the World Football League wooed Culp away with a tremendous bonus, a salary hike, and a pumpkin-colored Mercedes.

It wasn't always so complicated. Case in point: Jan Stenerud. He had been spotted as a college player by canny Don Klosterman before Don left the Chiefs. Bobby Beathard followed up for us and checked on the young kicker at Montana State. He came back ecstatic—just effusive. Stenerud had come to the United States on a ski-jumping scholarship, of all things, and, in storybook fashion, just happened to amble by a football practice as the ball bounced off the field. He kicked it back to the scrimmagers at the other end, who just stood there, stunned.

Our director of personnel, Tommy O'Boyle, and I jumped on a plane and flew to Oklahoma to see the boy play against the Tulsa Hurricanes. The young man was a lanky, blond Norwegian who looked like a serious athlete. He booted a couple during the warm-ups and it was abundantly clear he was good. Then, when it came time to kick off, Stenerud teed up the ball and lofted it high into the air, soccer style.

"Gees," I said, following its long flight. "Anything that goes that high and that far ought to have a stewardess on it."

The ball sailed and sailed, straight and true, right *through* the opposition's uprights—75 yards away and seven rows up into the bleachers beyond.

Tommy cleared his throat. "I did see that, didn't I?"

"That you did, lad," I said, nodding in disbelief.

A kicker will win or lose four to six games for you each season. What we were looking at was a man with at least six games safely tucked away in his toe. I knew right then and there that he was the guy we wanted, and we drafted him the first chance, sealing the bargain with an eighty-thousand-dollar bonus, a car, and a round-trip ticket to Norway.

Similar luck landed us kickoff returner and flanker Noland Smith. Scouting Tennessee State in just an intra-squad scrimmage, I noticed this extremely agile and fast runner. He was terribly good but not even on the Tennessee coach's recommended list. Too small, was the reason. But he was just too darn good, and I drafted him in the sixth round. "Super Gnat" proved to be sensational.

Sometimes a prospect was thought too small, and sometimes it was the school's size. Willie Lanier played middle linebacker for Morgan State, a little college overlooked by most pro scouts. It was too small, they thought, to produce serious talent. Our scout was an amateur in this instance and didn't know any better, I suppose. An ex-college player and career military officer, Frank Barnes had volunteered to scout ten eastern players for me. He was a good friend and not a man given to effusive compliments, so when he came up with an eleventh name, I sat up.

Willie Lanier was the best player he had seen the entire season, he said. Good enough for me. Lanier joined the Chiefs in camp and was an instant hit, a fast and crunching tackler. Nonetheless, Jim Lynch, another rookie, from Notre Dame, was assumed to be the leading contender for middle linebacker simply because he was white, and Willie Lanier was black. Sounds peculiar now, but there had never been a black middle linebacker in the pro ranks. It was as inconceivable as a black quarterback, I suppose. Hell, black players didn't even room with white players, much less call offensive or defensive signals on the field. Could an unheralded college player handle the pressure, given the unprecedented situation? I couldn't tell in advance, yet a lot depended on it. I did know one thing: He had the skill and the desire, and I was not about to pass on him because he didn't need to put blacking under his eyes to counter glare. I knew how something like that felt, firsthand.

I called them both in and told them point-blank that Jim was the more versatile and would be the outside linebacker opposite Bobby Bell. Willie Lanier was the middle linebacker of the Kansas City Chiefs. We needed them both to win, I said, but Willie had the middle.

Jim Lynch and Willie were elated. They couldn't have cared

less about middle or outside positions; they just knew they were rookies who were starters—first-string their first year! From that time on, they became fast friends. They also became room-mates.

Our Super Bowl loss made our needs painfully evident, especially on defense. We set about rebuilding for another go at the championship. Lynch, Lanier, Aaron Brown, Emmitt Thomas, Jim Kearney, and Jimmy Marsalis—these were the new generation. A couple of others I picked up jogging off the field one night with the coach whose team we had just defeated by two touchdowns. The two guys I wanted had done poorly in the game, and I sensed it was the moment to try for a trade. It was. The coach was displeased with Wendell Hayes and Goldie Sellers both. In a few seconds I had gained two more strong players because they'd had a bad night.

The NFL's highlight film of the first Super Bowl did not treat us kindly. I ran it at our training camp that July. Judging from the comments fired back at the screen, my people were angry at the narration and its derogatory tone. For six months they had taken the rap about our championship defeat, and it gnawed at them. They couldn't wait to play an NFL team again. That unlucky honor went to the Chicago Bears in the fourth exhibition game of the 1967 season.

We had lost the Super Bowl to the deceptive simplicity of the Packers' offense. We were, in their eyes, just fancy dancers trying to make up for our inadequacies with a lot of unnecessary and even unmanly razzle-dazzle. Plowing ahead, moving the ball forward, were all you had to do—*if* you could do it—the NFL champs seemed to be saying to us.

The Bears were charter members of the National Football League, and owner George Halas was a mainstay. The humbled Chiefs were the AFL president's personal team. The meaningless exhibition game was suddenly a grudge match.

The Chiefs pounced on the Bears with a vengeance. In the tight-I formation, Fred Arbanas, at tight end, shifted from one side to the other. Every time he moved, Chicago moved *six* defensive people. A quick count further added to their confusion. Dick Butkus, their great defensive leader, spent much of the game preoccupied with calling adjustments. He was more like a traffic cop than a middle linebacker.

On offense the Chiefs were merciless, running up 66 points against the Bears' 24, including a 99-yard touchdown runback by rookie Noland Smith. It was the worst shellacking Chicago had suffered in its fifty-year history.

It happened again in the last exhibition game. By then, word was out. The clash drew an awesome crowd of seventy-four thousand people, more than a regular season game or even the Super Bowl. It was a record attendance.

The opposition were the NFL Rams. We took them on in the Los Angeles Coliseum. At the half the Chiefs led 24–13. It was getting out of hand, even for a notorious exhibition-game winner like me. This couldn't go on. I didn't want the team to peak before the season, so I resisted my usual impulse and substituted freely. Rookies and new team members taxied in and out. I put in Pete Beathard at quarterback and gave him a long look too. The rest of the game we failed to score and we lost, 44–24. Team captain Jerry Mays was livid. I tried to mollify him. It was, after all, just a preseason meeting. Jerry shook his head.

"It wasn't *less* important than a league game! We won't play a more important one."

They wanted to redeem themselves and avenge the AFL for all the abuse it had taken from its rival league and the press. To bolster our forces, I traded Pete Beathard to the Oilers for Ernie "the Cat" Ladd, Jacky Lee, their quarterback, and a number-one draft choice. It was the biggest trade in our history.

The season began. We defeated Houston and shut out Miami before dropping one to Oakland by two tough points. Returning home for our first game in K.C., we trounced Miami again, 41–0. We were 3 and 1. San Diego roughed us up, and we moved on to face Houston. It was a bizarre game on paper. We had 19 first downs to their 9 and gained 323 yards to their 127, and we lost, 24–19. Their quarterback? Pete Beathard.

105

Still, the Chiefs' offense was downright explosive, I knew. In the next three weeks Lenny ignited them, and we blasted Denver, 52–9; the Jets, 42–18; and the Boston Patriots, 33–10. We were 6 and 3 on the season, we had a chance . . . until we met the Chargers.

The Chiefs ran out of gas. Seven times we were inside the San Diego 10 and couldn't put Mike Garrett over for a score. My mother could have scored with some blocking! Luck didn't abandon us, though. With nineteen seconds left to play, Jan Stenerud had the game cinched. He had only to kick the ball through the uprights from 24 yards out. He missed. Nothing was working. We lost by one point, 17–16, and our chance for a second championship went with it. The team was deflated. On Thanksgiving Day, four days later, we were beaten again, this time by the Raiders.

We won our last three games, to end with a 9–5 season, but it was academic. The Raiders were the AFL champs for 1967, and it was on Al Davis's shoulders now to even the score with the NFL in Super Bowl II.

Dallas was once again the runner-up in the other league, and Green Bay was once again the champ. The Packers were older and slower but much more experienced, and they all knew it was Vince Lombardi's last game as their head coach. There was no way they wouldn't win.

When he first took over the hapless, winless Packers, Vince had promoted their fourth-string quarterback, Bart Starr, to the starting lineup and led them into the history books with five league championships. This was their farewell performance for him, and they delivered, 33–14.

It had been fourteen years since I had met him in Stu Holcomb's office at Purdue. *"Lombardi! Not Lombardo. Lombardi! Lombardi!"* No one would forget that name ever again.

ELEVEN

NOW teams were being created, new franchises granted. League expansion. We lost Sherrill Headrick and Chris Burford to Cincinnati's new team, the Bengals. Bobby Hunt too. Chris called it a day and didn't report. I hated to see them go.

Things were changing. E.J.'s bum knees finally proved unable to sustain the punishment at linebacker, and I switched him to center. Only four players remained of the defensive unit that had started against the Packers in the Super Bowl two years earlier: Buck Buchanan, Jerry Mays, Bobby Bell, and Johnny Robinson. Seven remained of the offense. Mo Moorman was one of the new men; he moved into a starting position at guard. Robert Holmes went into the backfield. Eight Chiefs had been voted All-Pro honors. The team felt strong.

In Houston we edged the Oilers, 26–21, then lost a heartbreaker to the Jets by one thin point, 20–19. Joe Willie Namath gave us a breathtaking demonstration of control football for the final seven minutes of the game, starting on his 4-yard line. The kid was amazing. We recovered the next week and defeated Denver, 34–2, but that really wasn't indicative of our offensive strength. The truth was, we were sloppy and struggling. In the first half we led only 6–2. Lenny Dawson hadn't thrown a touchdown pass in all three previous games. I replaced him in the second half with Jacky Lee, who took the team the rest of the way.

Lenny seemed better against Miami, and we beat them handily, 48–3; yet he was shaky again the following weekend against the Bills and just managed to eke out a win, 18–7. The Bengals were the same story: We barely managed a 13–3 win. Granted, we led the division with a 5-1 record. Oakland and San Diego, however, were right behind, both within one game of the Chiefs. Obviously, one or both of them could rectify the situation by beating us. The Oakland Raiders were, in fact, our next opponent.

Otis Taylor was out with an injury, Gloster Richardson was doubtful, others were walking but wounded. Lenny was pressing. We needed something new to throw the Raiders off balance, cover our weaknesses, and allow us to maximize our strengths. Something new—a difficult proposition in a sport eight decades old. The I-formation had first been used around 1910; the shotgun, introduced by San Francisco, was a variation of the quick-kick formation. The T-formation had been around since the game's invention before the turn of the century. It had gone out of fashion, was dramatically revived when George Halas's Bears used it in 1940 to win the NFL championship over the Redskins' single-wing, then succumbed to the popularity of the pro set advocated by Jim Lee Howell's Giants in the fifties. Probably, I thought, nobody on the Raiders had ever even seen a T-formation, much less played against one.

I began sketching out the formation. Clark Shaughnessy and Ralph Jones were the ones who had refitted the T-formation for George Halas nearly thirty years earlier. They had added a man-in-motion component and counterplay. What if the Chiefs used a T with two tight ends for blocking, since our wide receivers were hurt, and used all three backs to block and run at the Raiders? About the last thing Oakland would expect from the Chiefs was a running attack to the exclusion of passing.

A Full-House T is what we called it, with Mike Garrett, Robert Holmes, and Wendell Hayes all in a line behind the quarterback and parallel to the line of scrimmage. The question was, how long would the Raiders stay surprised? Their coach, John

Rauch, was no novice, and Al Davis wasn't exactly a slouch either.

We sprang it on them right at the opening. It worked great. By the time the half ended, we were 17 points ahead. They hadn't even scored. We added another touchdown on the ground in the second half and beat them 24–10. My people had rolled up 294 yards rushing in sixty attempts and set a league record with eighteen first downs. Lenny had set one too. He threw three passes the entire game, completing two for 16 yards. That was an AFL first: the *fewest* passes thrown. The Raiders hadn't looked good; the Chiefs looked terrific. One of our two primary competitors had been beaten. Next on our schedule was the other, San Diego.

We knocked off the Chargers, 27–20, and with six weeks to go, the Chiefs led the Western Division. It was a tough game, though, and my people were hurting as we journeyed to Oakland for a rematch with John Rauch's legionnaires.

Certainly they were wise to our Full-House T, and the injuries that had prompted me to use it hadn't healed. We were going against them with the same problems and no new solution. The one edge we had was momentum: The Chiefs had won six in a row. I sketched out our standard I-formation, with the halfback behind the quarterback and the fullback behind the half, then put the split end beside the halfback as another runner. The Cock-I. One thing was sure—we were going to have to throw the ball.

Raiders quarterback Daryle Lamonica was in great form. They didn't call him "the Mad Bomber" for nothing. He connected for a 29-yard touchdown pass, set up a field goal with an 82-yard toss, and generally picked us to pieces. At the half, Oakland led 31–7. Lenny had managed one TD pass to Richardson.

Lamonica hit Billy Cannon for another score in the third. Lenny made a valiant comeback with a second touchdown throw to Richardson that covered 92 yards, which made it 38–14. Jacky Lee went in for us and threw a 61-yard TD, but the Raiders were too far ahead to be seriously threatened. At the gun the score was 38–21.

The Chiefs won their next five games, and we finished in a

tie for first place with the Raiders. The play-off was set for their stadium. Our guys were healed by now and confident; they had beaten Oakland once in the preseason, once in regular league play. In the final three games, Kansas City had racked up 94 points to the opposition's 20. We were having a great season.

But our play against Oakland did not reflect our confidence. It was just the worst, one of those games where I wished I could find some quicksand in their landfill stadium and exit quietly. We were flat—awful—and they beat us 41-6.

To win twelve out of fourteen games, log the best record in the team's history, and finish so ignominiously left me feeling empty. The year was over for us and I had no words to say.

I was the loneliest person on the flight back to Kansas City that night. It was after midnight; the next day was Christmas Eve. I had been voted Coach of the Year, and I was numb with disappointment.

The Jets beat the Raiders by four points for the AFL championship and qualified for the third Super Bowl. In two weeks they would meet the NFL's Baltimore Colts in Miami.

Nearly every sportswriter and commentator was picking the Colts, coached by Don Shula, as they had lost only one game the entire year. The contenders from the AFL were considered a fluke, and from an inferior conference, anyway, and their coach was the man Baltimore had ousted in favor of Shula. The gamblers, the press, and the NFL were not kind in their comments and predictions. The Falcons' coach, Norm Van Brocklin, went so far as to say: "On Sunday, Joe Namath will play his first professional football game."

Unfazed, Broadway Joe predicted victory and got in some digs of his own, but his was a lone voice. The Jets were as tired of hearing all the hogwash as we had been. They weren't awed, they weren't intimidated; they were plain determined and played a classic game. The upset was truly stunning, and among the millions of fans watching it across America on television, I knew the absolute happiest were the professionals of the American Football League, especially Jets coach Weeb Ewbank, formerly of the Baltimore Colts.

110

* * *

The fact that the Chiefs had achieved so much and gained so little ate at me that long winter. It had been a nearly perfect season. What more could I ask of them?

I instituted off-season workouts supervised by Alvin Roy beginning in March. The veterans bought the scheme, and the rookies naturally complied, so when they came to camp in July, they were already in good condition. I was especially pleased with Len Dawson. He had begun throwing hard five months earlier to build up his arm, and in the first month of training camp he was throwing the ball with midseason form. And he kept right at it. There were afternoons when he and Otis Taylor were the only two players on the field as they drilled through fifty pass patterns.

Our preseason schedule was six games, including four against NFL teams. We won them all. In the last one, though, Leonard hurt his hand diving for a loose ball. The abrasion turned out to be a broken finger. The Thursday before our first regular game it was swollen, and we discovered he had blood poisoning in his right arm as well. Luckily we caught it fast enough to counteract with injections, but his hand was too sore to take the snap from the center.

We figured out a way to overcome this by having Lenny reverse his hands underneath E. J. Holub and take the force of the snap with his left hand. On the flight out to San Diego, he soaked his bad hand the whole way, then soaked it four times daily up until Saturday. When I saw Len could bend his fingers, I knew he would play. Otis Taylor caught two touchdown passes from him, and we won 27–9.

I checked in with Father Mackey in Boston the following week, and he joined us on the bench as usual. We dominated the Patriots that game and were leading 17–0 in the third period, when Leonard rolled right on a pass play. A tackler hit him just after he released the ball, knocked him down, and rolled across his legs. Lenny limped out of the game. The doc checked him and couldn't find anything serious, just a bruise, and Leonard went back in the next quarter. When he took himself out shortly

111

afterward, I knew something was wrong. The leg didn't feel right to him, he said.

Jacky Lee finished up our 31–0 rout, and we boarded the flight home. Len's knee was wrapped in elastic, as the doctor hadn't found anything major, but now it was beginning to stiffen. Early the next morning I called him at home. He was hardly able to get out of bed, and the pain had kept him awake most of the night. I told him to go straight to the team physicians, Drs. Lichtor and Miller. They were to call me the moment they finished the examination. The diagnosis was disastrous: torn ligaments. It usually requires immediate surgery.

I prevailed upon the doctors to get a second opinion. We took Len to another man in K.C., and his diagnosis was the same. Two experts were saying operate, he has torn ligaments. I had seen a lot of knee injuries in my time, however, including my own at Purdue, and I just had a gut feeling the doctors were wrong.

In my sophomore year, practicing for the last game of the season, I heard a pop in my knee as I was tackled. The coach kept running "just one more play," and I continued to practice, fearing I might be benched. Like E.J., I sneaked off to the trainer for advice.

"If you heard a pop," he said, "I guarantee you tore a ligament. You had better put the knee in a cast right now, son."

I refused the advice and went back to the Sigma Chi house. That night I nearly cried myself to sleep from the pain. The next morning my knee was so sore and tender that I had no choice but to go to the team's doctor. He put it in a cast, as predicted, but he didn't operate, and the knee healed.

If Lenny had a chance to recover without surgery, I had to find it for him. An operation would finish him for the season. If this was going to be our year, we needed Lenny to make it happen. If his knee were put in a cast and began to heal, he could play in the stretch, when we needed him the most. Could we get a third opinion? Who was a top orthopedist?

I called Dr. O'Donoghue in Oklahoma City. He was at a convention in Buffalo. I reached him at the convention, and he agreed to examine Leonard in Oklahoma City the next day. The procedure would be done with Len under sedation. I cautioned the doctor not to do anything but examine him, as it was common to operate immediately if the findings warranted surgery. The doctor was put out. Such a request was highly irregular.

"I know it is," I said, my throat dry, "but this is a very unusual case. This man is very important to our team, but I'm more concerned for him as an individual. I don't want him to have an operation unless there is no other choice whatsoever."

The doctor called the next afternoon with the same diagnosis. I was 0 and 3 in the medical department. I prevailed upon the Chiefs' team doctor to get still another opinion, and we arranged for a second orthopedist to fly to K.C. to look at Leonard. He volunteered to fly straight to Oklahoma City to see Lenny with Dr. O'Donoghue there, but I said no. I didn't want to risk having his opinion influenced by the presence of the other man.

Dr. Reynolds arrived the next day. Lenny came by at noon. I had called him that morning to tell him yet another doctor was coming in. Leonard's wife, Jackie, arrived with him, visibly upset. I couldn't blame her. The head coach of the Chiefs was definitely resisting the collective wisdom of the medical establishment, shopping for a diagnosis to coincide with his own opinion. Why? I wanted to think it was as much for Lenny as for the team, but I wasn't sure myself. By then I was just caught up in the crisis, acting and reacting, pushing forward to try and do the right thing. The doctor put Lenny up on the conference table while my secretary took Jackie down the hall for a cup of coffee. Dr. Reynolds probed the knee and studied the X rays. I tried to read his eyes but couldn't detect anything at all. I didn't have a clue of what he was thinking, and he wasn't volunteering a thing. Did the silence mean I was wrong? Would he agree with all the other orthopedists?

Finally he straightened up and stepped back.

"Now, before I tell you anything, I'm going to say this to you, gentlemen. I studied under Dr. O'Donoghue, who is con-

113

sidered to be the finest orthopedic surgeon in the country. What I tell you will not be influenced by his opinion. It will be mine alone, and it is my opinion that your knee will respond to treatment and will heal without surgical intervention. If you do what I tell you to, and do not aggravate it, you should be able to play in about six weeks. However you must do exactly as I say."

I could have kissed him.

"There is no doubt whatsoever," he continued, "that surgery would be the safest and most sensible way to proceed. However, I realize you're a football player in the midst of a season, and there is a good possibility that the knee will respond to the proper therapy. Still, the decision is yours to make. It's your leg and your life." He looked at us in turn. "I'll leave you alone for a few minutes so you can discuss it together."

When the doctor had left, I looked at Lenny.

"Leonard, it's up to you. What do you say?"

"I thought you'd never ask," he half teased.

I smiled. He was right, I hadn't, not through four examinations. I looked at him closely. Leonard Dawson, fourteen years in the pros, four in the Big Ten, star high school quarterback of Alliance, Ohio. The face was older, the blue-gray eyes were the same. I had known him his whole adult life and then some, but I didn't know what he was going to say. I only knew what I wanted to hear.

I said, "I don't think you should get an operation if you don't need one. Talk to Jackie and let me know what you want to do."

Lenny shook his head. "I don't want the operation, Coach. We'll do what the doc says."

I was relieved. I also knew that if anything bad happened to Len Dawson as a result of this decision, I would never forgive myself.

Jacky Lee started in game three against Cincinnati, and the fates did their not-so-funny dance.

It was Jacky's hometown, and he did well. In the third period, we were leading 13–10 when Jacky Lee was helped off the field—his leg immobile, broken.

Mike Livingston, a rookie, went in at quarterback. We managed to add some more points with a field goal, but not enough to ward off the Bengals' fourth-quarter drives. They beat us, 24–19.

Monday morning I was on the phone, calling around the country for free agents who could help. The first one I came up with was Tom Flores of the Buffalo Bills. The second was John Huarte of the Jets. I signed them both.

Denver was the next club we would face. Flores and Huarte were cramming, trying to learn the Chiefs' system, so Livingston, an outstanding player, was the logical quarterback to go with, rookie or not.

The youngster would be nervous, of course; and the other two probably would be too. They needed someone to calm and encourage them, someone they would respond to. I called Lenny.

"Would you like to go to Denver with the team?"

"I sure would. I can't stand sitting around the house another week."

"The reason I ask is that I think it would help Livingston if you were on the sidelines, maybe give him some support. Some of the players mentioned it to me too."

"They did?" Lenny was delighted. I realized it would be as good for him to go as for the team to have him there. The presence of the team's number-one quarterback was an amazingly powerful thing, I knew, no matter who was actually in the game.

It wasn't going to be easy, I thought as I looked at the field in Denver. Half of it was frozen, and the other half looked like a mudhole. Then too the Broncos were a young, up-and-coming team, anxious to prove themselves.

Livingston went in at quarterback and handled himself well. He gained confidence as the game progressed and led the team to a 26–13 victory. It was the moment of truth, as far as the season went, and the Chiefs rose to the challenge. The kid deserved a lot of credit.

We blanked Houston, 24–0, in a driving rainstorm, with Tom

Flores throwing a 33-yard touchdown on a fake-field-goal play; and the following week we defeated the Dolphins, 17–10. Livingston was getting better with each game. Warren McVea, whom I had picked up in a trade, broke open our game against the Bengals with an 80-yard touchdown run. We beat them 42–22 for our fourth victory in a row. Lenny watched from the sidelines, reactivated and suited up.

Buffalo threw a lot of different defensive formations against us, and Mike Livingston had trouble reading them. The Bills led 7–3. I called to Leonard to crank up his arm: He was going in. He hadn't played in six weeks and I wanted him to get a feel for the game before the half.

It made it easier for him to start the second half. He looked good and put us ahead. Then, in the fourth quarter, the Bills' linebacker, Mike Stratton, blitzed. Nobody picked him up, and he hit Lenny high and solid. The vision of Stratton hitting Mack Lee Hill flashed through my mind. I held my breath as they unpiled, but Lenny bounced right up. He was fine. The Chiefs won, 29–7.

The following weekend we downed San Diego, 27–3, for our sixth straight win, a club record, and we were in first place. The Friday before our game in New York, Len's father died. Lenny played the game the next day against the Jets, completed twenty-three of thirty-eight passes, beat them 34–16, then left immediately for the funeral in Alliance. The respect his teammates had for him went up several more notches. If ever there was a team player, Len Dawson was it.

Four games remained, two of them against Coach John Madden's Raiders. We were 9–1 on the year, they had 8 wins, 1 loss, and 1 fateful tie. It was time for show and tell. We hosted the Raiders in Municipal Stadium in front of a record crowd of fifty-two thousand. The game was a bizarre cliff-hanger. Lenny was off the mark a lot and got intercepted five times, but he managed to keep it close. In fact, with seconds remaining to play in the fourth period, we were tied 24–24, and George Blanda ambled in and kicked a field goal to put them up 27–24. John Madden was elated.

We rebounded and beat Denver, 31–17, even with Lenny sidelined after the second quarter. He had hurt his knee a bit. Fortunately, it responded to treatment. Still, I kept him out of the Buffalo game, which we squeaked through, 22–19. That left us one game to play in the regular season: Oakland again.

The Raiders had a tremendous pass rush, and I worried about their getting to Lenny and that weak knee. It would have to be a war of attrition. I decided to go at them on the ground and keep the passing to an absolute minimum because, win or lose, we would have to play them once more, and that next game would be for all the marbles.

The Chiefs controlled the ball for most of the first quarter. The Raiders had it for only seven plays. One of them, however, was for 72 yards, a Lamonica-to-Wells bomb that resulted in a field goal and put the Raiders ahead by 3. Then it was back to the trenches. The game went scoreless for two periods. In the fourth the Raiders scored their first touchdown. The Chiefs fought back, running at the Oakland line, and finally connected for 6 points on a pass. The 2-point conversion was still in effect in the AFL. We decided to go for it. No good. The score was 10–6, with five minutes left. Now we needed another touchdown. The Raiders weren't about to oblige. They held the ball for the remaining five minutes and won, beating us for the second time. They were the Western Division champs.

The Chiefs were 11–3 on the regular season, however, and still had a shot at the Super Bowl, although the odds were long. We were in the play-offs. Our challengers were the Jets. They were the defending champions and dangerous, especially with Joe Namath. Their secondary was weak, though. Walt Michaels, the defensive-backfield coach, would probably go with four linebackers and three defensive backs to try to compensate. Up front their excellent defensive end, Gerry Philbin, had dislocated his right shoulder. He was slated to play anyway, which meant he would hit with his left shoulder first, then turn his body, at which point he would be susceptible to a good block. We would run at Philbin.

As for offense, I wanted us to control the ball and deny Namath as much as possible. The less he passed, the better off we would be. As I walked the field with Len Dawson before game time, the cold wind was swirling in strong gusts and I wondered if anyone would be doing much passing that day. Throwing the ball was going to be tough. Our punter, Jerrell Wilson, was warming up. He actually missed the ball with his foot as the wind gusted and blew it aside.

Sure enough, in the first quarter, Otis Taylor got loose and Lenny sailed the ball at him, but halfway there the wind took over and carried it just beyond the lunging receiver. Both sides managed field goals, but that was the only scoring in the first half. In the third period Stenerud hit on another field goal to lead 6–3, and Lenny found Taylor again, all alone. But the pass was taken by the erratic wind once more and flew far beyond the receiver. Two touchdowns blown away. I turned and looked at the sky in disgust. Father Mackey gave me a reproachful glance.

Draws, screens, and play-action passes kept the Jets' pass rush slow and cautious, but we weren't scoring. The defense was playing great, but how long could they keep Namath off the board?

The fourth quarter. Namath got hot. He threw deep to George Sauer in the end zone, but Emmitt Thomas knocked the ball away. An official's yellow flag came fluttering down (the guy must have tied a rock in it)—pass interference. The Jets had a first down on the 1-yard line. All they needed was a lousy yard.

They banged Matt Snell straight ahead and he didn't make it. Second down. Bill Mathis tried this time; he was stopped too. Third down, third down! We were going hoarse from screaming. The crowd roared as Namath rolled to his right. Snell slid into the right flat of the end zone, with our linebacker Bobby Bell in between him and Joe. Namath made as if to run, but Bobby wasn't buying the fake. He stayed on Snell. Joe finally ran out of field and out of time as he was brought down by a horde of Chiefs. Kearney, Bell, Lanier, Lynch, and Mays were on him. We had denied New York the touchdown with nothing but twelve inches between them and the goal—twelve inches and eleven determined pros.

I was never so happy to see a field goal by another team. They kicked and the score was tied, 6–6. It was up to the offense now. There was no more I could ask of the defense than they had already given. Lenny must have thought so too. He went out and hit Otis Taylor with a bomb—61 yards. We were on their 19! The field goal was there, but I wanted a touchdown. Lenny delivered it on the next play, a play-action pass to Gloster Richardson, and we were ahead, 13–6.

With ten minutes left, Namath had plenty of time, and he did in fact reach our 25 several times. But he couldn't pierce the defense for the touchdown, and there it ended. The Kansas City Chiefs were the wild card team in the play-offs against the Western Division champs, the Oakland Raiders, and the outcome of *that* game would decide the AFL's representative in the Super Bowl.

The merger engineered by Lamar Hunt would take effect the next season. All of pro football would be under the banner of the NFL. That meant whoever won the game in Oakland would be the very last champions of the American Football League.

TWELVE

"LENNY Dawson is involved in a betting scandal."

"What? You *have* to be kidding," I said.

Mark Duncan shook his head. Sent out by the league office to notify me, he had intercepted me at the airport in San Francisco as we arrived for the Oakland game.

He looked nervous as we drove toward the city. "We have a big problem, Hank."

"Mark, what the hell are you talking about?"

"We have it on reliable authority that a gambler, a restaurateur by the name of Donald Dawson, has been in contact with Lenny, and there is a big story coming out tomorrow. The league is trying to squelch it, but I don't know whether we'll be able to or not. Anyway, this guy Dawson is from Detroit and is a gambler and bookmaker, and he has been linked with Lenny."

"I can't believe what you're telling me," I said. "What do you want me to do?"

"You have to tell Lenny."

I groaned. "Gees."

"I know." Mark Duncan glanced at me as he drove. "It's a terrible time to have to tell him something like this."

If you only knew, I thought. The guy's got a glass knee, his father dies, he brings us to the AFL championship game, and now *this* for payment.

As soon as I got to the Mark Hopkins Hotel, where the team was staying, I phoned Leonard and said I had to see him right away, privately. He came right over immediately and I told him everything: that someone had apparently uncovered a big gambling scandal and that supposedly he had been contacted several times during the season by this gambler from Detroit.

All I wanted to know was if he knew the man and what there was to the allegations that he might have passed information about the team to a known gambler.

Lenny said he had met him when he was with the Steelers, through retired quarterback Bobby Layne. It was just a casual thing; he hadn't seen or heard from him again. The man had called to express condolences when Len's father died and asked about his health and his injured knee. That was it—extent of contact.

"Then there's nothing to the allegations at all," I said.

"Nothing whatsoever."

Lenny Dawson's word was good enough for me. I called Mark Duncan immediately and passed on what I had learned. Several hours later, he called back to inform me that the league office had succeeded in killing the story.

The workouts went well all week. The players were happy that we had come to California early, and it showed in their play. By Wednesday the heavy workouts were behind us and the game plan was in place. This time, with Lenny's knee stronger, we were going to pass more than we had in our last meeting.

Oakland had a tough secondary that excelled in man-for-man coverage, so we were going in with a number of different formations in order to take advantage of their single coverages. Their murderous tackle, Tom Keating, we were going to double-team with the fullback and tight end, working from our Model-T formation. Keating was the lock on their defensive wall, which we had to break open to spring Mike Garrett.

Would it work? The Raiders had defeated us twice during the season, but the games had been close—three points in one, four in the other. There was no denying that the odds were with them. Not only were they favored to win but the sports world was calling them the best team in pro football. They had been the Western Division champs for three years running.

After our light Friday workout, we moved the team to the Mark Hopkins Hotel in San Francisco. There wasn't much more to do but wait. Which is what Monsignor Mackey and I were doing in my suite that evening when the phone rang. It was a man purporting to be a great fan of the Chiefs. He and his wife, he said, had been out to dinner the night before and accidentally overheard a conversation between the Oakland quarterback, Daryle Lamonica, and somebody else. They were discussing the upcoming game, and in the course of the dialogue Lamonica had sketched out some plays on a place mat— new plays. When Lamonica left, discarding the sketches, the caller had retrieved them. He had them now. He wanted to give them to me.

I could practically see Al Davis's fingerprints all over this. It had to be Al. Whoever heard of a Chiefs fan in Oakland or San Francisco?

I was not about to fall for this setup. Still, the guy on the phone was convincing—too convincing. He said he didn't know enough about the technical aspects of the sport to fully appreciate the diagram, but it looked important to him. Al had to be behind this. Or else it was a hoax engineered by someone absolutely desperate for tickets to the championship game.

I thanked the caller and asked him to drop off the sketches at my suite at nine o'clock that night. There would be someone there to take them and give him some tickets for his trouble. He resisted accepting anything, but I prevailed upon him to change his mind. I hung up.

Mackey listened to the story of the phone call and made the obvious deduction: If it was a practical joke, it would be sprung on me when I went to the door to make the exchange. I couldn't possibly take the chance of opening the door to accept these "diagrams."

"You're right," I said, pacing.

"Then who is going to open the door and . . . ?" The monsignor stopped midway through the question.

"Right," I said, looking into his eyes.

"Oh, my God."

"Come on, Monsignor. Take off that collar and put on this shirt."

"Oh, my God."

"Come on. All you have to do is open the door, take whatever he gives you, and give him the tickets. That's it."

"Oh, my God," the monsignor repeated, then paused. "What if it's for real?"

"Exactly," I said. "Blow this and I'll put you on waivers."

For all his moaning, Monsignor Mackey carried out his role with the panache of a born skunker. Nor was there any surprise from the other side of the door when he opened it: no pie in the face, no message delivered in compromising attire complete with photographer and rubber chicken. Mackey carried the piece of paper back into the room and handed it to me. What sort of gag had we received from our anonymous guardian angel? I studied the crumpled place mat and was surprised to see expertly drawn plays.

I felt a twinge of empathy. It was the kind of doodling that players and coaches indulged in all the time. I did it myself, constantly—on envelopes, sugar packets, on napkins in restaurants. I even kept a pad and pencil next to my bed to jot down inspirations that might come in the night. It was an occupational obsession.

I called Tom Bettis and Tom Pratt, the defensive coaches, and summoned them to my suite. They agreed the drawings were too accurate to have been done by an amateur. The formations sketched out were brand-new ones the Raiders had never used before, in which Warren Wells, their best wide receiver, lined up in the slot instead of on the outside.

I swore the coaches to secrecy and instructed them simply to make the defensive unit aware of the possibility of such plays in our Saturday meeting before the Sunday game. We didn't want to disturb our overall plan or the defensive wrinkle we had added: Jerry Mays taking an inside route on his pass rush instead of making his usual attack from the outside.

Saturday night the team members enjoyed leisurely dinners throughout San Francisco and returned to the Mark Hopkins. John Madden took his people to a movie to take their minds off the upcoming game, then back to the Edgewater West Motel— in enemy territory, across the bay from our hotel. They were, I'd heard, already packed and ready to leave for the Super Bowl right after the game.

The next day we rode our chartered buses to the Raiders' stadium. After stowing our gear, Lenny and I walked the field together. The footing was good, although there were some soft spots inside the 10-yard lines on both ends. The weather was good, the temperature fifty-two degrees.

The Raiders kicked off. Lenny led the advance for two series, then unloaded a deep pass to Otis Taylor. It was well thrown but deflected at the last instant by the Oakland cornerback, Willie Brown.

Lamonica led the Raiders back at us and hit Warren Wells for a 24-yard gain. They were on our 3. Their back Charlie Smith waltzed it over, and Oakland led, 7–0. And so it went for most of the half. With three minutes remaining, Lenny brought the Chiefs to midfield and sent Robert Holmes into the line for 8 yards. It was the first time we had crossed the 50-yard line all day. Then Len unveiled one of our new sets and hit Frank Pitts, "the Riddler," for a 41-yard pass that took us down to the 1. Wendell Hayes slammed in for a touchdown and the game was tied, 7–7.

I had a feeling the momentum was starting to turn in our favor, and I told the Chiefs so at half time. I could feel their confidence.

In the third quarter, the Raiders went into a formation with Warren Wells in the slot, just like in the place-mat diagrams, and Monsignor Mackey and I exchanged conspiratorial glances. Oakland moved the ball, but the rush from Aaron Brown and Jerry Mays, Buck Buchanan and Curley Culp, thwarted Lamonica's passing attack. Three times they pushed inside our 33, and all three times they came away empty, missing even on field goals. Then we had the ball, but on our own 2-yard line, and it was quickly third down.

Lenny called the Camouflage Slot formation that positioned Otis Taylor between right guard Mo Moorman and tackle David Hill. Len scrambled around and spotted Otis Taylor, cutting toward the sideline. Taylor made an incredible catch on the 37 and stepped out of bounds. We were out of the hole!

If any one play changed the complexion of the game, that had to be it. We kept pushing downfield from there, and with a little over three minutes left in the period, an interference call put us on the Raider 7. We went for it twice and it was like playing against a brick wall. On the third try, Robert Holmes went in for a touchdown. K.C. 14, Raiders 7.

My heart was in my mouth at the beginning of the last quarter. We fumbled twice, and Oakland recovered both times, each one inside our 30-yard line. Twice Daryle Lamonica went for the quick touchdown, and twice he was intercepted by our cornerbacks, James Marsalis and Emmitt Thomas. Emmitt Thomas, from little Bishop College in Dallas, grabbed it on the 20 and raced 62 yards to their 18.

I told Lenny to keep it on the ground and burn some time. Jan Stenerud went in on the fourth down and kicked a field goal from the 22 to put us ahead 17–7, with a shade over four minutes left to play.

The last 240 seconds were agony, but the defense played brilliant football, and the Raiders didn't score a point. The 11-3 Kansas City Chiefs had beaten the 12-1-1 Raiders for the AFL championship of 1969. We were going to the Super Bowl.

E.J. emptied a whole bottle of champagne over Lamar Hunt that night on the plane ride home. What a flight! The stewardesses must have wished they were locked up in the cockpit with the flight crew instead of being trapped at twenty thousand feet with four tons of exuberant grid jocks and an entourage of coaches, owners, reporters, friends, and one Catholic priest from a Back Bay parish in Boston.

We landed, somehow, but there wasn't much time for further celebrating. We had to leave for New Orleans the next day. Unlike our first appearance in a Super Bowl, this one gave us only a week to get ready. Quite honestly, I preferred the shorter

period. Instead of having a horde of press in constant attendance, as we did the first time, interviews were limited to spe-
cific hours. I also had the team eat as a group at our headquarters
in the Fontainebleu Hotel, to serve as a reminder that we were
there as a team and for purposes other than the revelry going
on all around us as the town swelled with fans.

The only worries I had were Jim Marsalis, who had a kidney
ailment, and Johnny Robinson's cracked ribs. They were indis-
pensable, the kind of defensive backs who could turn games. I
was preoccupied with how to compensate for their possible ab-
sence when Mark Duncan called, the man from the league. The
betting scandal had come up again. In fact, it was about to break
nationwide on the seven o'clock news. The bookmaker from
Detroit had been indicted by the feds and had given names of
pro-football players with whom he had associated. Lenny's and
Joe Namath's were prominent among them.

"What do you want us to do?" I asked.

"The first thing is prepare Dawson. The media will be all
over him."

The hell they will, I thought. "What's the league's position?"

"The commissioner's office is working on a prepared statement, which we'll announce to the press sometime after the
telecast."

"What about Lenny? And what happens to our ball club
through all of this?"

"That's something you have to work out."

"Look," I said, trying to contain myself, "the whole thing is
simple. Lenny isn't guilty of anything and hasn't anything to
hide. The only thing to do is tell the truth, and the sooner the
better, because we have the Super Bowl to get ready for, and I
won't subject my people to something like this. It could turn
into a circus."

The rest of the day, after lunch, was to be devoted to watching films of our opponents with my four quarterbacks, and
coaches Pete Brewster and John Beake. Now I also needed to
sort all this out as well, and quick. I met with Lenny and told
him about the story that would air on NBC that evening, then
we looked at the films with the others. Undoubtedly the press

would soon hear about the upcoming newsbreak and descend on us. I couldn't leave Len alone from here on, and we couldn't keep running film forever. I sent the others off and asked Lenny to stay.

Our PR man, Jim Schaff, came by and said reporters were swarming all over the hotel looking for Lenny Dawson. The word was out. Schaaf had spoken to the league office several times, but they had no new information and just wanted us to sit tight. I grunted and reran the Minnesota films.

After the third viewing, I decided enough was enough. Len couldn't go to his own room, the media people and cameras would be there waiting. The best thing was for us to go to my suite by way of the stairwell. So we sneaked upstairs, and I sequestered Leonard in one of the bedrooms.

Frustrated and upset, I called everyone I could think of who might be of help in solving this problem. By late afternoon I had gotten exactly nowhere. I called the league headquarters and told them we were going to have our own press conference, with Lamar Hunt and Jim Schaaf, myself and Len Dawson.

That was fine, they had no objection to a press conference, they just didn't want any mention made of the betting scandal and the insinuations about Lenny's involvement.

"*Wait* a minute!" I said. "If we do that, if we ignore the thing they want to know about, then it will look like we're guilty."

"It's better if you don't say anything about the allegations."

"Hey! Lenny is not guilty, and we ought to tell them *just* that—that he's *not* guilty."

"We don't think that's the way to handle it, but it's your own responsibility. If that's what you want to do, you're on your own."

So what else is new? I thought. "Fine," I said. "That's what we're going to do."

They wanted the league's security people to talk with Len. I went and got him from the bedroom and asked him how he felt about it.

"It's all right with me. I have nothing to hide. Besides, I

want to find out what I'm being accused of in the first place."

It wasn't Lenny's, or Joe Namath's, first brush with such unwanted notoriety. Two seasons earlier, rumors in gambling circles about game-fixing had caused bookmakers to suspend betting on our games and had prompted commissioner Pete Rozelle to have Lenny interviewed by the league's security people. Their scrutiny was clinical and complete, including a lie-detector test that corroborated Len's complete innocence. That was wonderful on one hand and totally unhelpful on the other. The test was discreetly handled, as was only proper, and not even Len's teammates were fully aware of it. However, neither was the public aware of his exoneration because of the investigation's confidentiality, nor were the oddsmakers in Las Vegas apprised. So the investigation both helped and didn't help. Perhaps gambling rumors are by their nature insidious. It certainly must have seemed that way to Len on the eve of his toughest professional performance.

The latest insinuations added tremendous pressure that could easily undermine his concentration and cause mistakes. At the same time, they made every possible error the subject of suspicion and controversy. It wasn't a pleasant situation for Namath and the other players linked to this indicted restaurateur and accused bookmaker in Michigan, but their season was over. Leonard Dawson was at the apex of his career and standing in a national spotlight that was beginning to look like a bull's-eye. I felt for him.

"Okay," I said, gesturing toward the telephone.

Lenny picked up the receiver. Jack Danahy, head of the AFL's security department, wanted him down at the league's offices in the Roosevelt Hotel. I said no, absolutely not, because that's where the media people were staying. Danahy suggested meeting in his room before the full news story broke on TV that evening. I objected to that too and took the phone from Leonard.

"There is no way Len Dawson is going to do that, now or later. He stays with the team. I'm not going to disrupt the entire organization or get the squad upset over something they know nothing about. And I'm not going to have Len subjected to any more pressure. If anyone wants to see him, they'll have to come over here.

I didn't leave the security men much choice, but I didn't have much maneuvering room myself. The league news conference was scheduled for eight o'clock. Where did that leave us? We needed advice from people who knew the news game. I summoned three reporters I trusted: Joe McGuff of the *Kansas City Star,* and Cooper Rollow and Bob Marcus of *The Chicago Tribune.* I presented the situation to them in my suite, and all three agreed that holding a press conference was the right thing to do. Together we wrote the statement for Len to give. The conference was announced for eleven that night: late, as press conferences go, but I wanted the thing cleared up before another day began.

The seven o'clock network news carried the story that night: The Detroit restaurant owner Donald Dawson, who had been arrested by federal authorities in a Michigan motel room with nearly $500,000 in checks and alleged gambling records, had named four top pro quarterbacks among his acquaintances.

Pete Rozelle went on half an hour later, at eight, and called the report "totally irresponsible." The commissioner was putting himself between the accusations and the accused players to shield them and the league. Well done, I thought. A stand up guy.

We had dinner and worked on the statement, going over it word by word. It still wasn't finished at nine o'clock. Finally I suggested we just tell the reporters, straight out, exactly what we knew. Len would make his statement and leave without answering questions. They would have to understand that, given the circumstances.

At eleven Len Dawson went before the press. The room was jammed with journalists. He made his statement, giving the simple facts, and was escorted from the room. It went off without a hitch. The press people had heard it firsthand and accepted it as it was intended.

That night I stayed up until four A.M. watching films of the

129

Vikings. If I couldn't sleep, I might as well work, I thought. The more I watched the footage of Minnesota, the more confident I felt about our game plan.

The Minnesota secondary played receivers soft, almost 9 yards off. With the speed of our receivers, their defensive backs would back up possibly as much as 12 yards, so we could throw short in front of the Viking cornerbacks all day long.

Their two tall ends, Eller and Marshall, liked to pressure the passer with upraised arms. Double-teaming would keep them too busy fighting off the blocks for them to get their hands in the air. Still, they were big, and tough to run against to the outside. We would run inside.

Their great defensive tackle, Alan Page, occasionally lined up between the guard and tackle on short yardage downs, instead of between the guard and center. So he would be on the shoulder of our tackle, Jim Tyrer. Page had quick reactions. If Jim Tyrer pulled, Page would chase him along the line of scrimmage, and we could run a trap play to the inside. I watched Page at work several more times to confirm this, then put in a play based on it—65 Toss Power Trap. Then I turned my attention to our defensive line.

Mick Tingelhoff, their All-Pro center, was used to having a linebacker playing several yards off of him. That was the fashion in the NFL—a smart, relatively light center going against a linebacker. It was perfect for a mismatch. We wouldn't give him a linebacker playing him loose. We would give Tingelhoff Curley Culp to play with, head-on in an odd line. That would put either Curley, at 280 pounds, nose to nose with Tingelhoff, 237 pounds, or Buck Buchanan, 290. So their guards would have to worry about blocking the linebacker; their center would be busy.

Just to complicate life for Minnesota, we would use our triple-stack defense, with the linebackers playing behind the defensive linemen.

The odd line, stacked linebackers, and zone and man-for-man defenses—it was going to be a patented Chiefs defense. Same on offense: an I-formation. We had eighteen different sets and a great variety of plays waiting. If nothing else, Minnesota's renowned "Purple People Eaters" would know they were playing an AFL team.

They had nearly shut out the Browns in the NFL championship game, and Jimmy "the Greek" Snyder had them as thirteen-point favorites in the Super Bowl against us. This tough crew was led by a daredevil brawler at quarterback who loved to run with the ball himself, preferably over people—Joe Kapp. He had collided with the Browns' 240-pound linebacker and knocked him cold. "Zorba the Viking," his teammates called him.

Wednesday morning finally dawned. I gathered my team before breakfast, told them about the situation with Lenny, and tried to turn their attention toward Sunday. They sat quietly listening as I spoke.

"We've been in one Super Bowl and lost it. We have worked hard since March to get this far. The only thing that should concern you now is winning the game."

The room was silent. I cleared my throat and continued.

"We can't do anything about what was reported in the newspapers and on television. But we can do something about winning on Sunday. We all know Lenny is innocent. So let's direct all of our energies to doing a good job in practice. We don't have that much time left—today, Thursday, Friday, a light workout Saturday."

I looked around the room at their somber faces. What were they really thinking? Had all the negative publicity thrown them? Were they wondering if their quarterback would even be allowed to play on Sunday?

"Does anybody have any questions?"

One hand rose. It was E. J. Holub.

"You got a question, E.J.?"

"Yeah, Coach. When do we eat? And when do we get our tickets?"

THIRTEEN

IT was so cold in New Orleans that the water in the fountains around the hotel was frozen. Monsignor Mackey and I walked around the grounds, shivering in the frigid air. It was freakish.

I threatened to trade him to Minnesota, where the weather was always like this, if he didn't provide warmer temperatures by Sunday. He didn't laugh.

The workouts went well despite the cold, although Lenny was quieter than usual. By Saturday we were more than ready. Old friends and teammates called to wish us luck, among them Ernie Ladd. He had played with us the year before and was very popular with the guys. He said he still felt part of the team and wanted to be with us in more than spirit. I invited him to be with us on the sideline. He'd be there, he said.

By this time tomorrow it would be decided.

Phyllis and the kids had joined me, and we were in the suite when Ed Sabol called. He was an old friend and the president of NFL Films. Instead of wishing me luck, as I expected, he insisted on seeing me immediately.

"Ed, I have no time now. My sister is here, my mother, and a lot of guests. Talk to me on the phone."

"I can't. It's too important to discuss over the telephone."

He wouldn't even tell me what it was about, just that he had to see me *now*. Within twenty minutes, he was sitting in the living room. It wasn't private enough, he indicated, and we went into another room.

"Let's hear it, Smush. What do you have that's so important?"

"Hank, I want you to listen, and I want you to listen very carefully." He paused for dramatic effect. "I want to wire you for sound tomorrow."

"Sure," I said, incredulous. "You're crazy. You mean to tell me that you came over here to ask me *that*?" I held my brow, feeling around for where the headache was going to originate. "Wire me for sound in the Super Bowl, the biggest game of the year?"

"You heard me," Ed said.

What a week, I thought. "Listen, Smush. This isn't a good idea."

"Hank, Hank! The only documentation we have of a coach in a major game is of Knute Rockne. Everybody loved that footage, but it was complete fiction."

"Yeah, I know, Ed, but we're talking about the real thing, and the Super Bowl no less. Do you know what this *means* to us? To me?"

"Exactly, exactly. Nobody has ever heard what a coach in a big game does and doesn't do, or how he goes about orchestrating the game on the sidelines."

"But Ed—"

"You've been lucky, Hank. Football has been good to you."

I rolled my eyes heavenward. "Ed—"

"Football belongs to the fans, and you should give something back to them. You should allow them the opportunity to see you in action in this Super Bowl game. You owe it to the fans of pro football."

"Why are you asking me? Why don't you ask the Vikings' coach?"

"Number one, Bud Grant isn't animated on the sidelines.

Number two, I don't think Minnesota is going to win the game. And Number three, you don't use profanity.''

"Damn right," I said.

Ed rumbled right on: "We can't just take a chance with anybody. We've tried this in the past with others and had to cut out practically everything because of the bad language. You're my *only* decent chance to do this, Hank. Please!''

"All right, all right. But I've got a condition.''

"Anything. What?"

"You have to promise me that I have the final decision on whether or not it's to be shown. Fair enough?''

"You got it!" Ed was joyous.

"Okay. So how are you going to work this?"

"Simple. We come in two hours before the game and wire you. By the time the game starts, you'll have forgotten all about it. The only thing you have to be careful about is that nobody else knows what we're doing. It's got to be as natural as we can possibly make it. Nobody's gonna know—not Phyllis, not Lamar Hunt. Nobody but you, me, and the cameramen.''

"I won't say a word."

"Great. It's going to be a half-hour special, so make sure you win.''

I threw Ed out just as Lenny dropped by. He had come from the player's final dinner together. Most Saturday nights they were on their own. This Saturday I insisted they take their meal together in the hotel, just to be safe.

Leonard looked composed, although a little thin. The pressure was making him lose pounds. I knew he was eating his heart out, but he never showed it. You would've had to know him for a long time to see that the gambling story was getting to him. His teammates and the press called him "Lenny the Cool," and he was. He never let anything affect his playing, not even me. That day in New York, playing on his frail knee against the Jets for the league championship and probably thinking about the news of his father's death, Lenny had failed to appear on the field for a special-situation team he was on. We were left a man short and I had fined him the mandatory five hundred dollars. His teammates were no doubt aghast at this. Not Lenny. He understood: The rules were the rules. He beat the Jets with a brilliant performance and flew home to bury his dad. But this gambling thing was different; it was working away inside him. The biggest day of his life coming up, and this had to land on him.

We chatted aimlessly. I think he just wanted company. Will he make it? I found myself wondering. Can anyone take this much pressure?

I looked at the face of the kid I had known for twenty years and saw a middle-aged athlete staring back with a look of anguish and determination, a pro quarterback with a shot at the world championship who wasn't going to let anything stand in the way, not even his own pain.

At breakfast the next morning the White House called. President Nixon wanted to wish us luck and asked me to pass along his confidence in the integrity of our quarterback. He wanted me to tell Leonard he said so, that nobody believed that TV news story.

We boarded the buses for the stadium and waited for the police escort. It was slow in coming. I didn't want the waiting to cause any nervousness, so I had the drivers proceed without the escort. When we arrived at Tulane Stadium, we ran into another delay. The security people were hesitant about letting us through. E.J. once commandeered a bus we were on in a similar situation, and teammates were urging me to loose him at this bunch when the guards waved us through. I looked at the guys as we drove on. They weren't nervous, I saw. *I* was nervous.

When we got to the dressing rooms, Ed took me into the empty trainer's room and put a transmitter underneath my shirt and a microphone behind my tie, where it wouldn't be visible.

The team had gone out to the field to look around, and I wanted to see if they liked their small surprise when they returned to suit up. Several days earlier, the league office had

135

asked me if we would allow an emblem with the seal of the AFL to be sewn on each jersey of the game uniforms. I thought it was a great idea and readily accepted. When the guys saw the emblem, they lit up. It was amazing how strongly they felt about their lame-duck league.

Then Ernie Ladd walked in. A howl went up. Everybody was happy to see him and surprised by how changed he appeared. He was wall-to-wall hair—mutton chops, moustache, beard. The works. He looked like an Oakland Raider. The fellows were making a big fuss over him and teasing him about all the hair, when he walked over to hug me and say hello.

"Ernie," I said, "if you're going to be on the sideline with us and a part of this football team, you'd better look like this football team."

The guys howled.

"Oh, man, Coach, don't tell me that I have to shave this moustache and beard and everything off. I'm a professional wrestler now, and it's part of my act."

"You decide what you want to be. Do you want to be on this team and look like us, or do you want to be a wrestler? If you keep the ornaments, you can't sit on the bench. If you shave it off, then you're with us."

The players broke up. They began kidding Ernie, egging him on to use the razor. He went into the shower area and began shaving. When he came out, he made a big show of demonstrating his handiwork to me.

"How's this, Coach?"

"That's a good start. Just keep hacking until you get it all."

He went back in and returned a few minutes later.

"This has *got* to be okay, Coach."

"Much better," I said, "but you have to take it *all* off."

The team cheered. I had never seen them looser before a game, any game. Ernie went back to the showers. When he came back, he was slick as a whistle. I mean, cleanly shaved. Everybody was laughing and applauding, and Ernie made his way around the lockers, laughing too. He had given them a big lift.

Amid the noise, I motioned to Monsignor Mackey. "Let's go check the track," I said.

The weather bureau had actually posted a tornado warning, but it had stopped raining, the temperature had gone up, and there was no sign of a twister. I had heard, however, that there were some holes in the tarpaulin and that the field was soggy in some places, so I wanted to test the turf. Mackey was nice enough to accompany me in this only partially useful errand. The truth was, there wasn't much you could do about bad patches except be aware of them. Mostly, he was there to humor a nervous coach and keep him busy.

The Minnesota Vikings and the Kansas City Chiefs took the field for the NFL-AFL championship. Actor Pat O'Brien, who had played the lead in *Knute Rockne—All-American,* recited "The Star-Spangled Banner" to Al Hirt's trumpet accompaniment, and joined us on the Chiefs' bench. As Monsignor Mackey walked past him with his hands in his pockets, O'Brien beckoned him over.

"Are you saying the beads, Monsignor?"

Mackey gave the aging actor a huge smile. He pulled his hand out of his pocket to reveal his rosary beads.

"That's good," O'Brien said. "That's good."

It was January 11, 1970, and the Chiefs had come back to the Super Bowl. The stadium was filled to the rafters with eighty-one thousand people. Back in Kansas City, the streets were deserted. The crime rate plunged, and electricity usage surged fifteen million watts over the norm, as everyone hunkered in front of their television sets to witness the kickoff. The game was under way.

Nothing much happened. The two sides felt each other out. Jan Stenerud drew first blood with a 48-yard field goal that I hoped would unnerve some of the Vikings. Two more kicks added more points and we led 9–0.

Stenerud kicked off, and the Vikings fumbled. Suddenly we had it on their 19-yard line. Two runs went nowhere, then Otis Taylor made a big third-down catch to put us on their 4, goal-to-go. We were 4 yards from a touchdown.

Minnesota dug in. In sixteen games, only four touchdowns had been scored on them on the ground. *Four.* Our first crack at their wall put us a yard back from where we'd started. The next shot was for no gain. These guys were tough.

It was third down and a short 5 to the goal. We *had* to have the touchdown. Their right tackle, Alan Page, had penetrated really well in the previous short-yardage plays. It seemed the right moment for the 65 Toss Power Trap: the 60 series, number 5 hole; Toss, meaning the tackle would pull out of the line as if to block for an outside run; Trap, as in Page. Tyrer would bait the trap, Mo Moorman would close it. If Page lined up between Tyrer at tackle and our guard, the odds of its working would be even better. The Vikings didn't cheat this way often, just once was what we were praying for. Sometimes you guessed wrong, sometimes you guessed right. I sent the play in.

Lenny broke the huddle and brought the team to the line. Page set up between our guard and tackle. If he took the bait now, we had him. The ball was snapped. Tyrer pulled, and Page pursued along the line. Mike Garrett took the hand-off from Lenny and disappeared into the left side.

I could see only Lenny, still faking possession, his back to the action. Then the crowd roared. Without even turning to look, Len clapped his hands together and smiled, and we both knew it was a touchdown.

Sixteen to nothing. It was the only time Page would set up in that position the entire game. We had caught the Vikings and sealed their fate.

Minnesota was famous as a second-half club. I warned my people of this at half time and told them they had to play as if the score were zero to zero. K.C. controlled the ball for the first six minutes of the third quarter but had to surrender it. The Purple Gang fought back. They marched 69 yards and vaulted into the end zone, making the score 16–7. If they scored again, we would lose the momentum.

The Vikings kicked off, and the Chiefs bogged down. We faced a third and 8 on our own 20-yard line. The Minnesota ends were great leapers and reacted to the flow of a play very aggressively, so misdirection plays worked. Would the Vikings take the bait one more time with a reverse play older than their grandfathers? What the hell. We tried it one more time, and it worked! Frank Pitts got to the 30, then a holding penalty moved us to the Viking 46 with a first down.

Lenny called the signals. E.J. snapped the ball and retreated. Minnesota's safety was blitzing! Len barely acknowledged it, but I knew he had read it. Coolly he hit Otis Taylor on a quick 6-yard hitch on the break. Otis caught it in front of their defensive back, Earsell Mackbee, gave him a move, and was gone. Mackbee was on the ground, pounding the earth, as Otis raced for a touchdown. Kansas City 23, Minnesota 7.

The hairline crack Stenerud had opened with his field goals was now a chasm. They were beaten. The defense took it the rest of the way, shutting down the Vikings' rushers and shutting out their pass receivers. Typically, even with the game grinding down, the Chiefs played like hell, knocking Minnesota's quarterback out of the game in the final quarter.

With two minutes remaining, I took Len Dawson out. He had thrown twelve completions out of seventeen for 142 yards and a touchdown, and he had called a brilliant game. I wanted him to hear the roar of those eighty thousand people, and they graciously obliged as he trotted off. I stepped out across the sideline stripe and onto the field so I could be the first to greet him and shake his hand. He had been superb.

The clock ticked away the last two minutes of the American Football League's existence, and I thought about my ten years with the Chiefs, the three league championships, the Super Bowl lost, the Super Bowl won. I looked up at my wife and my six kids, my mother, Mackey beaming on the sideline, the players hugging and congratulating one another, elated. How lucky I was to have had a second shot at this, I thought, because no other of the AFL head coaches was still coaching with his original team. I had lasted ten years. Somewhere up there was Lamar, and I was happy for him too.

The gun sounded.

It was over. Ernie Ladd and Otis Taylor, David Hill, Emmitt

Thomas, and the others picked me up like a cupcake, and carried me across the field. The Kansas City Chiefs were the last champions of the AFL and the world champions of professional football. It was an unforgettable moment.

I cupped my hands around Leonard's face in the bedlam of the locker room and half shouted that the president of the United States was on the phone and wished to congratulate the game's MVP.

Lamar was ecstatic. The coaches were embracing everyone. Tommy Bettis and Tom Pratt, the defense coaches; Bill Walsh, the offensive-line coach; Pete Brewster with the receivers; John Beake with the backs; Alvin Roy; Wayne Rudy—a great staff.

E.J. said, "I hope Joe Namath and the Jets are as proud of us as we were of them last year."

Tommy O'Boyle, Bobby Yarborough, Ed Buckley, Lloyd Wells, and Joe Litman were downright gleeful. We had done it!

The celebrating went on but slowly the players managed to shower and primp for the team party at the Sonesta Hotel in the French Quarter. They went off into the hollows of the stadium, their voices echoing back the elation.

Finally it was time to leave. There wasn't anyone left except Monsignor Mackey and I. I noticed no one had bothered to pick up the Super Bowl trophy. There it stood, in the corner of the room, a silver football atop a silver stand. Mackey went over and picked it up, cradling it in his arms like a baby.

"Wow," he said. "Wow."

We went back to the hotel and changed clothes, then collected friends and family and went over to the team bash. By the time we got there everyone was well into it. I got carried around the room like a matador. It was a great blast. We partied for what seemed like minutes but must have been hours. I was so happy and excited, there was no way I was going to sleep.

Out on the sidewalk, I told Phyllis we were going to Al Hirt's place.

Even at that hour there was a long line to get into the club. We did an end run and went to the back door. Al's son let us in and showed us to the main room. The place must have been filled with Kansas City fans, because they started yelling, "Hank, Hank, Hank!"

Al Hirt cupped his ear. "Is Hank Stram really up there?"

The customers yelled, "Yeah, yeah!" and Al signaled for the stage lights.

"Hank. Come on down."

What a great night.

FOURTEEN

THE next morning at the huge press conference, I was still excited. The Chiefs were vindicated; they were the champs. We had finished the job begun by the Jets in the previous Super Bowl. No doubt could remain in anyone's mind about the level of talent in what would henceforth be called the American Football Conference of the NFL.

Somebody wanted to know about future trends. I said the sixties was a decade of simplicity but the seventies would be a decade of variety. The days of the quarterback staying in the pocket were over; he would have to be able to move. Likewise, the I-formation, now used only by Dallas and by us, would become dominant. Stacked linebackers would be used more, as would zone defenses.

We had used the triple-stack against the Vikings for 95 percent of the game, and they had had a difficult time adjusting. Conversely, on offense, our multiple formations had confused the defenders. Quick counts and camouflaged receivers had thwarted their readings of our formations. They couldn't find their keys fast enough because they were unaccustomed to what they were seeing, unaccustomed to a different kind of strategy. We had created a moment of indecision and that was all we needed.

Some of the reporters pushed me to say something about

Lombardi, something vindictive that would make good copy. I deflected their leading questions and stuck to broader issues. To no avail, I noticed the next day as I read the sports pages.

"LOMBARDI SYSTEM PASSE"—STRAM read one headline. Another piece declared the Kansas City formations "the offense of the seventies." I winced, knowing I would be hearing a lot of jibes about that one. Still, I didn't care. I was just too happy.

Back in Kansas City, 160,000 people turned out to welcome the team home. As had happened in Dallas, we had given the city its first professional sports championship, and the citizens were wild with joy.

Requests for speaking engagements and appearances poured in, as did awards. Coach of the Year awards were presented in Washington, New York, Los Angeles, Chicago, Honolulu, Baton Rouge, Detroit, Palm Springs, Dallas, Jacksonville, Minneapolis. Johnny Carson had me on *The Tonight Show,* and I appeared on *The Ed Sullivan Show* and *The David Frost Show* as well. The league meetings were in Hawaii, and Lamar was nice enough to invite the entire Stram family, all eight of us. Al Hirt even flew out to play at our victory party.

When I got back from the trip, Al arranged a luncheon in my honor in New Orleans, emceed by Bob Uecker. Afterward, Al and his wife and Phyllis and I were the guests of Governor McKeithen. In fact, we stayed at the governor's mansion. It was clear then, as it had been in Hawaii, that Al Hirt, minority shareholder in the New Orleans Saints, was promoting me to the majority shareholder, John Mecom. Mecom went so far as to say that I could have a salary far bigger than what I was getting in K.C., as well as equity in the team. It sounded too good to be true, but then I couldn't believe I was a guest in the Louisiana governor's mansion, either.

And the Saints weren't the only ones. George Halas's son, Mugsy, flew into Kansas City and broached the subject of my possibly coaching the Bears. For a guy born in Chicago and raised in Gary, it was a very exciting thought. But I had a contract with the Chiefs that I had to honor before I could begin entertaining such dreams seriously.

There was a team to coach, and the time for basking in the warm glow of our Super Bowl victory was running out. March rolled around, our minicamps started, and we had to prepare for the draft. It was amazing how fast it all went by. Reality also made a return appearance in the form of Ed Sabol of NFL Films. As promised, he flew me to Philadelphia to screen the film they shot of me on the sidelines—complete with sound track. I groaned when I heard myself extemporize. In the heat of battle my remarks about the opposition may have been understandable, but I wasn't at all sure I wanted to share them with the whole world. There was one crack about the Viking defenders running around in confusion as if they were doing "a Chinese fire drill," and there was also an unkind observation about passes the secondary was conceding us.

I pointed these out to Ed and asked him to delete them. Smush made a great display of his willingness to abide by our agreement about this. But he also made a big pitch about the integrity of the thing, and how that really was my true sweet self up there on the screen saying those things. People didn't know that's the way I was, he said, but he played tennis with me, and golf, and knew that I was always needling somebody and always talking a lot. Great, I thought, but do I really have to have myself revealed in this manner before millions of TV viewers? Everybody, Ed insisted, thought it was gritty and real and just super.

At the black-tie premiere in Kansas City, I cringed. There I was, chastising officials, belittling our opponents. When the Minnesota quarterback lofted a soft pass, I heard myself say, in stereo, "Boy, it looked like there was helium in that one."

When the house lights went on, I wouldn't even go to the stage. I had paid for my seat, I figured. Ed predicted that the film would become a classic, viewed by more people than any other the league would make. He was right. The film aired on network television in May and was quite a hit (but no other coach, to this day, has agreed to submit to a similar venture).

The new season was bearing down on us fast, and I had one last bit of unfinished fun to take care of after our world-championship season. Every player, of course, had received that most-coveted prize, a Super Bowl ring, complete with name, number, position, a ruby for the K.C. team colors, and lots of diamonds. Coaches got them too.

I had cuff links made in the exact same design and presented sets to Chuck Baer, my high school coach; Stu Holcomb, my last head coach at Purdue; Terry Brennan; Matty Bell; Andy Gustafson of the University of Miami; and Monsignor Vincent Mackey of St. Cecilia's Parish in the Back Bay of Boston. I owed them more than I could ever say, and I wanted them to know it.

Just to make things interesting, the players went on strike. The other teams had training camp to worry about, but the Chiefs also had a game to play: the All-Star Game sponsored by *The Chicago Tribune*. The Players Association had ordered their members not to report to camp—only rookies had been exempted—so our veterans were practicing on their own at a high school field across town, while the new recruits and the rest of us were at our regular training facilities at William Jewell College in Missouri.

The standoff became a crisis when *The Chicago Tribune* threatened to cancel the traditional contest between the top college players and the top team in pro football. Other players around the league were pressuring the Chiefs not to participate. A lot of our people very much wanted to, yet they didn't want to betray their colleagues either. Nothing was happening.

I figured I had to do something quick; the clock was running out. I ordered a helicopter in Kansas City and had the pilot set me down right in the middle of the high school field where my guys were practicing. It certainly got their attention, as I had hoped.

"Gentlemen," I said, "the All-Star Game is not a part of the new season, it's an extension of last year's. It's a prize for winning the Super Bowl. You owe it to yourselves. If, after the game, you want to go back on strike, that's fine. But I want all of you to take a vote and make your decision—right here and now, because time is getting late."

The game was only eight days away. The Chiefs voted to

play. We went to Chicago and won, of course, and then the players dispersed and went back on strike. Still, they took a lot of criticism from other pros and there was a bad feeling around the league about it, since the game had broken the strike. It was a feeling that would come back to haunt us later.

The strike was settled. Our first preseason game was our very first ever against the Dallas Cowboys and everyone rose to the occasion. Beating them 13–0 just made Lamar's day. He invited Mackey and me to the newest and most expensive restaurant in Dallas to celebrate. Things looked deceptively good. Then they started coming apart.

We didn't play with any consistency once the regular season began. We dropped the opener, beat Baltimore on the road, and lost to the Broncos in Denver. And so it went, like the stock market, up and down. Amazingly, we still had a chance to win the Western Division championship with two weeks to go, providing we beat the Raiders and the Chargers. We lost both.

We had spent a great deal of effort preparing. Winning the Super Bowl had been a great challenge, but winning it again was what it was all about.

But something went out of the team, and we didn't repeat as world champions or even as conference champs. The season ticket sales were excellent, the crowds were boisterous, the Chiefs were a success, but something had changed and something was missing.

What? It bothered me deeply. We and the Chargers had inaugurated off-season training. The Chiefs had been the first team to utilize Nautilus machines, under the tutelage of our strength coach, Alvin Roy, and the first to establish minicamps. Hell, we had won the All-Star Game with only eight days of work because of the conditioning program. The problem wasn't physical readiness. So what had gone wrong?

During the season I had told the team time and again that some way, somehow, we had to find a way to win and not an excuse to lose. In this dark hour, I could only conclude that I had failed to sell the team on finding a way to win.

FIFTEEN

IT was a new season, 1971, and I was back doing what I loved—coaching pro football. The routine had become a part of me, as had the Chiefs, so it was particularly hard to take the news that season.

Jerry Mays called the house, sounding troubled. Phyllis gave him the number of the store where I might be shopping, and he reached me there. Jerry's father was intending to run for mayor of Dallas and wanted him to take over the family's construction business. He had an obligation to his dad and had to retire, even though he didn't want to and certainly didn't have to at his age.

It was an awfully tough thing for an athlete in his prime who loved the game. It was tough for his coach as well; he was irreplaceable. I tried to talk him out of it—and failed. Jerry Mays, "Mr. Huzzah," captain of the Kansas City Chiefs, had hung up his shoes.

E.J. decided it was time too. E. J. Holub, after ten years of leading and cajoling, was going back to Texas for good. Knowing he wouldn't be playing anymore left me with a feeling of emptiness. The "family" was breaking up, each going his separate way.

We lost our opener on the road and flew home. By the time

I reached the house, the films of the game had already arrived. I took the kids and Phyllis out to dinner, then brought them home and sat up for a couple of hours, studying the film.

Monday morning I checked in to the office at seven, bringing with me the cans of film for the rest of the coaches to look at. Aside from practice, we spent a long day analyzing our mistakes, making corrections, noting the good and bad things our players had done, and scoring each of them in every conceivable area of performance: from his stance to downfield blocking, to play execution, pursuit, et cetera. The ratings were then posted.

Practice followed the meetings, paperwork and mulling followed the practice. By nine that evening, I was home. For an hour or so I watched the Monday night game reported by Frank Gifford, Don Meredith, and Howard Cosell.

Tuesday and Wednesday were long, tough days. The team would see the films of their win or loss and begin studying the footage on our next opponent. We'd hold practice then go back to working on our offensive game plan. None of the staff made it home before midnight, usually.

On Thursday the defensive game plan would go in, reflecting everything we had been able to learn about our opponents: their tendencies on first and 10, second and long, second and short, third and long. . . . It also condensed to manageable proportions our strategy for winning: the plays to set them up for the play that would burn them for a score, the formations that would—we hoped—confuse their backfield, the pass patterns that might work against their defensive secondary and linebackers. The goal was to come up with ten or twelve major plays, scoring plays. If we hit on three or four of them, that would give us the 21 or 28 points with which we generally believed we could win, provided the defense did its job.

Friday we would look at more film, hold a light workout, and get home early. Saturday too. Then would come the game, and the cycle would begin all over again: arriving home to find the film waiting.

After our opening loss to San Diego, we won the next five.

Then came the Raiders. With about four minutes left to play, we led 20–17. Lenny was scrambling for what would be a long gain, when Ben Davidson tackled him high at their 17, and a couple of other guys jumped on. Otis Taylor got upset at the pileup and leaped on a Raider. A fight ensued. The ref slapped the Chiefs with a foul that put us out of range of even their goalposts. Oakland got the ball back and moved it close enough for George Blanda, the old wolf, to kick a 48-yard field goal in the final three seconds that tied it up, 20–20.

I raced to the officials' locker room right after the gun, furious with them for the penalty call that had scotched the win for us. I couldn't remember being so outraged by a ref's call. Bill McNutt followed me in, fearing trouble, and escorted me back after Cal Lepore had calmly explained their logic.

We were still downcast when we lost to the Jets the next week, but we took the next two before dropping a Thanksgiving Day game in Detroit. Then came a Monday night game in San Francisco on nationwide television. We beat the 49ers 26–17 and won the last two games, to finish the season with a 10-3-1 record and the Western Division championship. That put us in the first round of play-offs against the Miami Dolphins, who had exactly the same record in the East.

Don Shula's club was a tough, new expansion team that had risen to the top of the Eastern Division. One of their specialties was blocking field goals and extra points. They did it by overloading one side of their defensive line, then blasting in to leap in front of the kick. We thought we might exploit their trick with a gimmick of our own—a fake kick. Instead of Dawson, the holder, getting the snap, the ball would go to the kicker, Jan Stenerud. Not many people were aware that he could run the 40 in 4.6 seconds, and with somebody chasing him, it was impossible to tell how fast Jan might go.

The game was played in Kansas City on Christmas Day. I was hoping for typically cold weather, but it turned out to be 62 degrees. The first two times we had the ball, Jan kicked a field goal and Lenny connected with Ed Podolak for a touchdown, giving us a 10–0 lead. On our third drive, we got to their

22 and stalled. With the ball on the right hash mark, it was time for the fake field goal.

Jan was going in with the play. I cautioned him to make sure he looked like he was going to kick.

"Remember, Janski, you have to do a good acting job. Don't squeal the play. Just watch the spot on the ground where the holder would normally put the ball, and you'll see the flight of the ball as it comes back to you. Once you catch the ball, run! Run like hell. You'll have two big blockers in front of you. It'll be an easy touchdown."

Stenerud went in with Bobby Bell, who centered. Lenny would audible the play at the line of scrimmage, depending on the Dolphins' alignment. On all snaps we used Bobby Bell, who was excellent at accurately firing the ball back to a kicker or holder.

Bobby leaned over the ball, looked between his legs, and saw Stenerud staring at the ground. In front of Jan knelt Lenny, hands extended for the fake snap. Everything was perfect—except instead of going to Stenerud, the ball was snapped to Dawson. Lenny and Jan were stunned for a fraction of a second, but they recovered and instinctively made the kick attempt. Amazingly, it missed by inches. Meanwhile, the guards had pulled out to the right and were now standing alone on the right flank, the touchdown in front of them.

"Bobby!" I said to the center as he came off. "*Why* didn't you snap it to Jan?"

"I was afraid he had missed the automatic. He just didn't look like he was expecting the ball. I didn't want to take the chance. So I snapped it to Lenny."

What could I say? It was reasonable, but instead of scoring a touchdown and pulling away to a 17–0 lead, we had given Miami a chance to come back. And they did. Late in the game we were tied at 24–24. Then Ed Podolak made a tremendous kickoff return of 78 yards to the Miami 22, with a minute and a half left.

We ran a couple of plays to set up Jan, and on the last play he went in for the 31-yard kick. Everything was good, except he missed by a hair, and we were in overtime.

In the first overtime period, we had another crack at a winning field goal, but it was blocked. In the sixth period the ball finally flew through the uprights, except it was Miami's Garo Yepremian doing the kicking, and the Dolphins won 27–24. The only thing we got for our trouble was joint billing in the record books as having played in the longest game in history: three hours, twenty-two minutes, forty seconds.

In truth, it was a draining defeat. Podolak had had the game of his life: 350 yards. Hell, the team had run up a total of 606 and lost. It was the best team I had ever coached, I knew, and yet we didn't make it to the Super Bowl. That was a lousy way to finish our stand at the old stadium on Twenty-second Street, where we had been the winningest pro team in football for the last five years running.

I felt terrible. It was a real heartbreaker, and I went to Florida to put it behind me. Dan Devine called to ask for advice—should he consider coaching in the pros? He had a tentative offer from the Green Bay Packers. I said yes, and explained to him the advantages in great detail. Some weeks later, prior to the Super Bowl, I ran into the president of the Packers, Don Olejniczak, and accidentally learned that he had called the Chiefs. He'd wanted permission to talk to me about my becoming the Green Bay head coach and general manager.

"Didn't they tell you?" he said.

I shook my head. "Nope." Lamar had never said a word.

Everything was getting bigger, more layered, and more spread out. A new $43 million state-of-the-art stadium was built for the Chiefs, true enough, but even that seemed part of a huge expansion involving the Chiefs and Lamar Hunt that was dwarfing the team organization. We were going into the stadium business in a big way: concessions, parking, luxury boxes, corporate suites. Seventy thousand season seats had been sold, and we hadn't even moved in. We were big business.

Lamar was diversifying too, investing in a theme park for kids and families and in sports ventures like World Tennis and the Dallas Tornadoes soccer team. Winning and losing gave way to profit margins and overhead. Priorities changed—drastically—and it was clear that the new corporate order wasn't overly pleased with what it perceived to be the easy access to Lamar Hunt enjoyed by the Chiefs' head coach.

With all the hoopla surrounding the move to Arrowhead Stadium, the team itself slipped out of focus. Princelings in the organization were of the opinion that a winning tradition had nothing to do with the building of the new stadium. Look at Washington, Chicago, New York, they argued. They hadn't won titles in years, and yet they filled their stadiums every week. The "cost justification" wasn't there.

I was beginning to have some misgivings, but I hoped things would settle down once everyone got over the excitement of the new facility. A vice-presidency and ten-year contract was offered by Lamar; I signed it and felt reassured. I would be head coach until 1981. Except for one or two other pro coaches, such tenure was unprecedented. Even so, I didn't feel comfortable being head of a corporate division called the Chiefs, nor with being part of an organization with another division called Worlds of Fun, the amusement park.

When the stadium was going up, I had expressed my preference for artificial turf, given the predictably foul weather conditions in K.C. We wound up practicing on the synthetic surface as well. When a lot of the players asked for a grass surface to train on, since it would be easier on their legs, the request I made was turned down. My recommendation to put the equipment man on straight salary instead of having him live on a contributed sum pooled by the players was also rejected, even though he had been with the team for a decade or more. Other proposals to better the team's lot were similarly turned down, and I found myself feeling disgruntled. Where once we would have done whatever was necessary to improve the team and its working conditions, that priority had now been forgotten—discarded. People no longer spoke, they sent memos. The bulletin boards groaned under the weight of them.

Jack Steadman, a former Hunt Industries accountant and now the Chiefs' general manager, was rising steadily in the consortium burgeoning around the success of the K.C. Chiefs and was beginning to speak with authority on the subject of pro football. Jack was a good bookkeeper. However, he was not good with people and he had the ability to say the wrong thing at the wrong time in the wrong way. He didn't know the first thing about football or players, nor should he have, given his financial background. My understanding with Lamar was that I ran the Chiefs and that no one would ever interfere with us concerning anything related to the team. This didn't seem to sit well with Steadman. It didn't help matters that I didn't often agree with him, didn't take his football insights seriously, or that I had teased him once about his gridiron acumen.

I was watching a game film when Jack appeared. He gasped at the passer on the screen and expressed his astonishment at how the man was able to throw with his left hand, since Jack was sure the player was right-handed. The film was in the projector backward. But I couldn't resist the opening and said the passer was ambidextrous. Didn't Steadman know that this quarterback threw with his left when rolling left and with his right when rolling right? It was patently ridiculous, of course, but to my surprise, Jack Steadman oohed and ahed and apparently bought it. He literally ran to his office to call Lamar and related his astonishing discovery. He told Lamar their quarterback was going to revolutionize pro ball.

Could a football team really be operated like an MBA program? I didn't believe so. You can't take the game and the fans for granted. But our K.C. corporation seemed to think that all you had to do was pump up the balls and screw on the helmets to keep winning. Teams are people, and football is a people's game.

My prosaic attitude prompted speculation in the corporate corridors that I was too close to the players, too emotionally involved, and that therefore I wasn't drafting and trading and cutting ruthlessly enough. I was keeping the older players on past their usefulness. Perhaps they thought world-class athletes could be ordered up like a sandwich or a spare part, and that teams worked like committees.

I sat in my office and mulled. In a pile of old stuff, I came across one of Lamar's notes, one of the hundreds he seemed to have sent over the years. Often they would be written on the margin of a news clipping he thought pertinent. This one was on a postcard. It was his suggestion for the team picture. On the card he had drawn outlines of heads and shoulders, with numbers on the jerseys. He suggested that we have the team line up in numerical order instead of by position. There was something silly and sweet about the idea, and I had always kept it. Now I wondered if that same wide-eyed Lamar was still in charge, even half as involved as he had been when we first picked out the equipment and the team uniforms in his living room.

To cool off, Phyllis and I decided to try a relaxing cruise aboard the *Queen Elizabeth II,* $90 million worth of luxury liner, to get away from it all, as they say in the brochures. The first night out we hit a storm. I got seasick, and the ship's boilers broke down. We were becalmed, adrift in the middle of the Bermuda Triangle—helpless.

It went on for three days. Finally we were rescued. A reporter asked for my reactions to the cruise. I said it was great. Surprised, he asked if I would recommend an ocean voyage to others. I said definitely: John Madden and the Oakland Raiders.

SIXTEEN

BY the '74 season, we were experiencing another strike and a downward slide as a team. The front office had grown more distant and less responsive, and a lot of players had checked out. Mo Moorman had packed it in and bought himself a beer distributorship in Louisville. George Seals quit to become the first black member of the Chicago Board of Trade. Willie Lanier would take a job with a tobacco company and retire after the season. I tried to talk him out of it.

"Coach," he said, "I just don't have the drive to play football anymore. It doesn't mean nearly as much to me as it did before. It's time for me to get out of the game."

The Chiefs had squeaked to an 8–6 record in 1972 and slipped to 7–5–2 the next year. By 1974, the fans were becoming vocal about their expectations. We weren't meeting them—or mine.

The World Football League had come into existence and was going after talent. They had signed a strong player of ours, Curley Culp. I tried to keep him with a salary hike and the biggest signing bonus in the team's history, but to no avail. He wanted to get out of Kansas City because of his asthma and to play in his home state of California. Not unreasonable, I supposed. But then he broke a small bone in his hand against Pittsburgh. It was nothing that would have prevented him from playing the rest of the season, as Jerry Mays had in '69, but the trainer reported that Culp had removed himself from the next game's roster, saying he would play but only if we provided extra compensation for the risk.

I confronted Curley in my office, and he confirmed this. I don't think I was ever angrier at a player in my life. He wouldn't have to worry about playing defense against the Dolphins, I told him. When he left, I called the Oilers and offered him in a trade for John Matuszak. Believing the World Football League would never get off the ground, the Oilers accepted the deal.

The team played its heart out against Miami in an incredibly tight game, which we were leading 3–2. No one could understand why I wasn't playing Culp, and I hadn't told them. I couldn't bring myself to do it, and it was a mistake. I should have. They were bitterly resentful of my keeping him out because so many of our starters were out with injuries. In the last minute of play Larry Csonka crashed over the goal line for the game's lone touchdown.

We needed a lift. We were going to play a Monday night game, and I needed to raise the team's spirits. I put in a call to a friend who came ambling over toward the end of a practice session a few days later. He was yelling and hollering, grabbing players and acting like he was going to fight them. What a sight. I have never seen anybody attract as many people as Muhammad Ali, or a person more compassionate and sincere. Talk about a great human being.

It was amazing to see all those professional athletes light up. They were proud champions once, he told them, and recognized around the country as the very best of teams, and they could recapture the title again, with sacrifice and dedication.

"Say, why is that big fella wearing all that equipment? What kind of stuff is he wearing? You know, I go into a fight, and they pull that stool from under my black ass, and I gotta go out there and *fight*! And these guys got all that help. Man, it must be *fun* to play football."

He was great. We beat Denver in Denver on the nationally televised Monday night game (maintaining a streak on that program that would eventually come to nine wins out of ten appearances). It didn't ultimately help, though. Lenny was getting on, as pro athletes go. He had elbow trouble now, and it was at the point where we had to literally count every ball he threw, especially late in the week, so he would be strong and fresh enough for the game.

Our last home game was against the Vikings, and we lost 35–15. We were 5 and 9—our first losing season in a decade. I was feeling really low when Lamar came into the dressing room. He invited me to dinner with several other people, but I felt too lousy and begged off. He nodded sympathetically.

I went out to the East-West game to scout for players and was having lunch at Ricky's in Palo Alto with the Patriots' coach when I got a message to call Lamar. I missed him and said I would call back from the high school where the teams were practicing. An hour later I called, and Lamar got on.

"Oh, lad," he said, mimicking my Frank Leahy imitation, "this is a very sad day in the history of Kansas City Chiefs. I've decided to make a coaching change."

He was serious, of course, but how serious?

Lamar flew to San Francisco to meet me. Eight o'clock at the Hyatt on Embarcadero Center. When he arrived, he said he wrote better than he talked, and handed me a memorandum. I stared at it and read, ". . . *we find ourselves in a very crucial time period for pro football and the various individual franchise operations. I have some very substantial obligations in relation to the stadium. . . .*"

I suppose the bland wording was intended to soften the shock, but it only made it seem worse to be told you weren't really being fired, you were just . . . leaving. Fifteen years, 210 games, and a memo.

You know going in that eventually you are going to be fired. You work for somebody else in a volatile business, and that somebody has the authority to do what he wants, whenever he wants. It doesn't matter what the reason is, because it's his team, his money, his football. He has the prerogative. I thought

157

Lamar had made a wrong decision, but what guy doesn't when he has just been let go?

I told him he should change the name of his club to the Kansas City Memos. I wasn't walking away, I wasn't quitting. I was being fired. As I wasn't resigning and had seven years to go on my contract, they had an obligation to honor.

The announcement was held, at my request, until I could get back to Kansas City and tell my coaches. I flew back and broke it to them after seeing Lamar one last time in Kansas City. After nine consecutive winning seasons and a losing season, I was out. No other pro team, except Cleveland, could match that record in that period. Eight play-off games, five wins. In fifteen years we had won 124, lost 76, tied 10. Three league titles and the world championship. We had won more games than any other AFL team, and I was the only head coach who had gone the distance, lasting the entire ten years of the league's existence. The fans wanted another championship, of course, and grumbled, but the stadium seats were full, even on the road, and the team would evolve as the generations of players changed over.

I was proud of what I had done, proud of the people who had played for me, and I was out. I sat in my office and began cleaning out my desk.

Buck Buchanan came in and stood over me. When I got up, he just embraced me. Lenny came by, Otis Taylor, Jim Lynch. I ducked the news conference announcing the "change" and went home. Some of the players stopped over with their wives. Cosell called, and Ali. What a guy. He is exactly what you see—probably the most generous and loving person on earth. Norma Hunt, Lamar's wife, called in tears. She said how sorry she was, and that I would always be the Coach. I told her that the first time I had seen her, I knew she was the No. 1 draft choice. She laughed.

When everyone had gone and the phone finally stopped ringing, I saw Phyllis off to bed and went to the den. Lamar Hunt was wrong, damn it. He had panicked.

I looked at the pictures of my kids. Mary Nell, named for my

mother and Phyllis's; Dale, for Purdue quarterback Dale Samuels; Julie, for Julie Rykovich, a childhood friend from Gary
who had played for Notre Dame and the Bears and the Redskins; Stuart Madison, named for coaches Stu Holcomb and
Matty Bell; Gary Baxter, for my hometown and a dear priest,
Father Baxter; and Henry Raymond, my eldest, named for me,
of course, and Ray Schalk. Ray . . . I had met him at Purdue,
he at the end of his career in baseball, me at the beginning of
mine. Hall of Fame catcher, lauded by Babe Ruth, fifteen years
of playing and coaching his heart out for the Chicago White
Sox, and fired in the space of an afternoon.

Ray was a happy, wonderful man, but whenever the subject
of his termination came up, his eyes would moisten and he'd
turn away from the memory of it. He had gone on, and so would
I. In a way he had prepared me for this.

I paced the room worrying what the Chiefs might do to con-
tinue rebuilding, how I might help. Then I realized I had to
stop. I'd been cut.

SEVENTEEN

I signed a broadcasting contract with CBS and wondered if I would ever coach again. The break had been abrupt after twenty-eight seasons.

As the summer schedule of exhibition games neared, I began to get excited and also a little worried. I had no training in television journalism. The network set me up with a coach and I flew to New York to meet my tutor.

"We're going to film you, and all you have to do is look into the camera and pretend you're doing a game. Just talk naturally."

I followed the lady's directions and sat with her afterward as she made her observations.

"Your voice is good, and so is your timing. It's also obvious you know the subject matter. However, you've got to be aware when the camera is on you. Make sure you look into it. Don't stray. Don't have nervous eyes. Just remember one thing above all—be yourself." She smiled. "You're ready to go."

Could this be all there was to it? I asked my boss, Bob Wussler. He told me not to worry. To get my feet wet, I asked to do some exhibition games, and that was arranged. Other than one gaffe, I managed to get off to a good start in my new career with the help of an experienced sidekick, Bob Halloran.

The television work lessened the emptiness I felt over not being directly involved with football for the first time in my life. To improve my broadcasting performance, I applied some old techniques. I recorded my reporting faithfully and replayed it on a tape machine I kept in my car. I would listen to my broadcast and wince when I made a mistake or spoke too fast. Slowly I learned my lessons and corrected myself. Perhaps because of the twelve years I had spent as an assistant coach up in the press box above the stadium, I felt at home in the broadcast booth. I was liking it, a lot.

For obvious reasons, I wasn't assigned to Chiefs games, until one day when the New York Giants were scheduled against Kansas City at Arrowhead Stadium. I was assigned to the game with Al Michaels.

It had been almost a year since I had last set foot in Arrowhead, and I was nervous all week long. It felt strange driving back to the stadium on the day of a game. I settled into the broadcast booth and was surprised and delighted to see friends and players drop by to wish me well. I was really touched, and even a little taken aback, when the last one came in. Lamar Hunt shook my hand and wished me luck.

Al Michaels and I did an exceptionally good job that day. We were able to call a lot of plays from the booth that were right on the money, and that was really gratifying. "When you see the red light go on, start talking." That was basically the training I had gotten, but thanks to guys like Al, Vin Scully, Curt Gowdy, Dick Stockton, Chuck Milton, Bob Stenner, Chuck Will, and Gary Bender, I managed to get through those early days and learn the job as I went along.

Things weren't organized in quite the way I was used to. We had staff meetings on Saturday, but frankly, they never really accomplished anything. A coherent approach wasn't taken until Terry O'Neill came into the picture. Terry had a definite idea of what a telecast should be like, and he made sure we all knew it. He wanted us to be prepared—to get as much personal information as we could prior to each game so that we could humanize it for the audience.

My routine was not unlike the one I had followed in coaching, and Terry had formalized our duties. Everybody had to be on location by Friday and at practice Saturday, to talk to the coaches, talk to the players, look at the game films. I even talked to the equipment managers.

Phyllis loved our new life. We actually got to have lunch together. The kids were happy to have me around more too. Then, one day in October, the phone rang.

John Mecom, the owner of the New Orleans Saints, wanted me to take over as head coach.

Louisiana. It was a beautiful part of the country, and I loved it. It was also serious football territory. Before they even reached high school, kids around Louisiana would play contact football with full uniforms and equipment, but often barefoot in the warm Gulf sunshine.

The Saints' quarterback, Archie Manning, was a mover and had a terrific arm. However, the team was doing terribly. Even so, the temptation to build a new team was too great to resist. I took the job and the following season began recruiting coaches. The draft was kind to us. We got Chuck Muncie from the University of California, a powerful runner with good speed, and a terrific blocker and receiver named Tony Galbreath. "Thunder" and "Lightning" were their nicknames. New players and free agents were lining up fast. The only question mark was Archie Manning, who was recovering from a shoulder operation. (The injury was serious and persisted. He never played a down for us in 1976.)

Before training camp was over, owner John Mecom was making his displeasure known in the most counterproductive manner, giving interviews about his complaints to the press that were inevitably seen by the very team we were trying to build and boost out of its slump. When I confronted him about it, he said it had been done "in jest." Clearing the air didn't help either. In fact, the subsequent news accounts of Stram making Mecom "eat crow" were additionally destructive.

There was something not right about this. I had been advised against taking the job and now I was wishing I'd been more prudent. We finished the preseason 4 and 2 and lost our first 2 games to strong teams, Minnesota and Dallas. Our next game was in Kansas City. There was a lot of hoopla about it in K.C., but I tried to downplay it as just another game, no matter how much I wanted to win this particular one.

It was odd staying at a hotel in K.C., for now I was a visitor. Once the game started, I got wrapped up in the action. The game was tight. We were leading 20–17 with under a minute remaining when I signaled for a time-out. I sent in a play-action fake with a flanker on the right side. Bobby Scott executed it well and hit Henry Childs in the end zone. We beat 'em 27–17. It was only the third game of a long season, and there was a long road yet to travel in building this team, but it was gratifying to start on that journey in Kansas City.

There was some implied criticism from the press in the dressing room afterward that I had wanted to pour it on at the end. They were right. I had wanted to do it, and I did. There was no reason to pretend otherwise.

That win had to last me for some time. The Saints did not fare well their first season, finishing 4 and 10, yet at least it was 2 wins more than the previous season. Encouraged by our showing, John Mecom presented me with a gold Rolex watch at Christmas. Nonetheless, every instinct told me it was going to be a rocky path with him. Everything around Mecom was so unpredictable; one second he could be lauding you, the next minute he would be inexplicably disparaging and untrusting. One thing I knew: The success of a football team had to begin with the quarterback. If you didn't have it there, you didn't have it. We did what we could to beef up the lines, and we prayed for Archie Manning to heal.

He performed well in camp, and we won five of our exhibition games, but right at the end of the preseason Archie sprained his ankle and looked doubtful once again. He was a great competitor, however, and started against the Packers anyway. He nearly did it too, losing only 24–20 after trailing by 24 points. The following week we lost less gracefully, to the Lions—though again by 4 points, 23–19. I was unhappy about the way we had lost and brooded about it on the flight home. The team was somewhat downcast as well, and the plane was silent.

Then Mecom began to go back and forth, from his seat to the player's area. A coach, then a player, came to me and told me he was making wild accusations to the team about their play and about the game plan. I tried to remain cool, since there was nowhere and no way to talk to John alone until we landed. But the comments continued and grew loud enough for me to hear. Enough was enough. I took the papers off my lap and went straight to Mecom. Straddling his legs, I pointed my finger right in his face.

"John, if you have something to say, say it to me. Don't say it to anybody else, because nobody can do anything about it but me. Now, what is it you want to tell me? What the hell is bothering you? Because you're upsetting my staff and my players."

Mecom immediately did a backstroke, but I knew the situation was too peculiar to last. The die was cast. Less than two seasons into the job, I knew there would be no job very soon. I wasn't even upset, just bewildered.

In February my assistant coach, Dick Nolan, was named to my position. With the talent we had assembled, the Saints went 7 and 9 that season, 8 and 8 the next, then plummeted to 1 and 15. In 1985 John Mecom sold the Saints and called it quits. It was the end of a tumultuous era for the New Orleans team, which had never seen a winning season during Mecom's tenure.

I picked up with CBS where I had left off, and I never looked back.

EIGHTEEN

WE didn't do badly, Jack Buck and I, covering preseason and regular-season games on television and radio. In 1978 we took over the radio coverage of the Monday night games being covered by Howard Cosell and company on TV. We started with 650,000 listeners, modest by most standards, and by 1984 had built up the audience to 10 million. It became the in thing, in fact, to watch the game on television *and* listen to it on CBS radio. We were going strong when the contract lapsed. The competition won the new one, and Jack Buck and I started a new show, *The NFL Tonight*. Things change, especially in football.

When the Kansas City Chiefs won Super Bowl IV, the team had six coaches. The minimum today is eleven, and some squads have thirteen, so you've got as many people on the sideline coaching as there are people on the field—or even more. In a critical situation a quarterback will go over to the sideline and talk to the offensive coordinator. Meanwhile, the head coach is at the other end of the bench, kicking artificial turf.

On the far side of the field, on the opponent's sideline, the middle linebacker is conferring with the defensive coordinator while the head coach is examining the synthetic blades of grass by his toe.

It's hard sometimes to tell what a head coach contributes. I know this, though. The ones who win consistently are deeply involved with their teams and organizations, and they *coach*. Don Shula, Bill Walsh, Mike Ditka, Tom Landry, John Robinson, Berry, Noll, Knox, Tom Flores, and others are head coaches in the true sense, and it shows in the results of their work. Their names are synonymous with winning, with performance.

In 1960 the player limit was thirty-three; now it's forty-five, sometimes forty-nine. All clubs now have at least two team doctors. Each front office, once consisting of an owner and a general manager, now has as many as nine people handling the operations of the organization. Even the number of officials has risen, from three to seven.

Playing and coaching used to be a six-month job, but the demands of the increasingly competitive game have made it a year-round one.

Players are bigger and yet faster. Where once we talked about 4.6 or 4.7 speed, now 4.3 is the impressive standard. Weight training, once frowned upon as debilitating, is today commonplace.

Kicking used to be casually, carelessly run through on the Saturday before a game, and rushing the kicker was unthinkable. Today special teams are coached by expert coaches in the nuances involved in all the various special situations. Most dramatically, there was, when I started in football, *one* alignment on offense and man-for-man coverage on defense. Now different alignments abound and there are *hundreds* of contingencies to be anticipated from them.

The game changes. Today we are in an era of specialization and situation substitution. Instead of eleven men "going both ways," or even eleven defensive starters and eleven offensive players, we have platoons of specialists trudging in and out of games constantly, as the tide of battle produces different strategic problems. Why haven't we seen more of the no-huddle offense that could foil and exploit this by preventing such substitutes from bringing in their special talents?

No one has done it yet, but I'm sure it will come. Because football, like life, is about change.